JOHN PAUL II
and the
MEANING OF SUFFERING

JOHN PAUL II
and the
MEANING OF SUFFERING

Lessons from a Spiritual Master

BY ROBERT G. SCHROEDER

Our Sunday Visitor Publishing Division
Our Sunday Visitor, Inc.
Huntington, Indiana 46750

DEDICATION

To Sarah, my wife, and my mom and dad,
whose faith and courage amidst suffering
have been an inspiration.

And to my precious children,
Elizabeth, Dominic, Bobby, and Sam,
who have filled my heart with the joy of fatherhood.

TABLE OF CONTENTS

INTRODUCTION

None of us can avoid the sting of suffering. Regardless of our age, race, religion, occupation, or IQ, suffering is always there following us around like a black cloud that rains down misery. It hurts us and the ones we love. It shakes our spirit and scandalizes our hope. It reminds us of the evil in our midst and our need for liberation.

As people of faith in a God who gives meaning to our lives, we struggle with the senselessness of suffering. Suffering doesn't always work like we think it should, striking down the wicked and sparing the good. Bending the laws of justice at whim, suffering victimizes who it wants to — even the most innocent among us — without hesitation or conscience. Such absurdity often leaves us wanting for any black-and-white explanations for our pain. And it seems the more we try to unravel suffering's mysterious ways, the more they slip through our mind's grasp and elude our search for meaning. Yet our hearts still cry out for answers.

Questions

- Why does a loving God allow us to suffer?
- Did we do something to deserve our suffering?
- Does our pain serve any purpose in God's plan?
- Can faith give us any reasons to hope?

These are the questions that rack our minds and jab at our souls. They press down hard on us to respond and leave us wondering: are there any real answers that can help us cope with the trials and tribulations of yesterday, today, and tomorrow?

In unison with the entire Christian tradition, Pope John Paul II replies in the affirmative. We can indeed find meaning in suffering — provided we look for it in the treasury of divine wisdom fully revealed in Jesus Christ. As the Second Vatican Council has stated, only in Jesus do "the riddles of sorrow and death grow meaningful."[1] This Christian conviction that faith sheds light on the deep mystery of suffering means that it is right for us to seek answers in hope. For only in searching can we find the Gospel, or good news, that Jesus' life, death, and resurrection give saving meaning to our many sufferings in this life.

Lessons from a Spiritual Master

John Paul gifted the world with a beautiful meditation on this saving meaning of suffering in his Apostolic Letter, *Salvifici Doloris* (Latin for "Saving Suffering"). The letter, the subtitle of which translates to English as *On the Christian Meaning of Human Suffering*, was dedicated February 11, 1984, on the Feast of Our Lady of Lourdes. With the wisdom of a spiritual master, the authority of the Vicar of Christ, and the compassion of one who has known intense suffering himself, the pope takes great care in this document to teach us what the Church believes about suffering. In its pages, we find a modern-day gospel on suffering — a message of good news and hope to all who stand scarred by the past, wounded by the present, and fearful of the future.

I first stumbled onto this letter twenty years after its writing, during a time in my life when I was deeply hurting. Having just celebrated two years of marriage to my wife, Sarah, I was slowly recovering from an illness that incapacitated me for ten months. At the same time, I was grieving the death of two of our children to miscarriages. Sam, our first baby, died six weeks after he was conceived; Bobby, our second child, died five months after conception and had to be delivered at the hospital.

In the wake of these personal tragedies, I felt consumed by suffering, which sent me headfirst into a downward spiral of sorrow, confusion, and anger. So I turned to my faith — the rock upon which I have tried to build my life — to help me find meaning in my pain. Over my thirty years as a Catholic, I had heard many spiritual quips from the pulpit about "offering up suffering," "sharing in the suffering of Christ," and "uniting suffering to the Cross." But to me, these ideas were like skeletons without any flesh on their bones. What exactly did they mean, where did God reveal them, and how could they help me get through another day? Hungry for answers, I consulted the Bible, as well as Christian books and articles, with the hope of finding sustentative spiritual food. But the cryptic sayings and sometimes superficial explanations of suffering that I read seemed irrelevant to my personal circumstances.

It was at this critical juncture that I discovered John Paul's *Salvifici Doloris*, which led me in a direction of healing. As I read the letter and allowed myself to become the pope's student, I came to see the Christian meaning of suffering in its full light for the first time and found insights into many of the questions that were disturbing my spiritual peace.

Make no mistake — this act of opening myself to the wisdom of John Paul and the Church through study and prayerful reflection didn't make my suffering vanish, but it did help me understand the truths that God has revealed about suffering. In doing so, I was able to gradually replace the heavy burden of despair I was carrying with the lighter yolk of Gospel hope.

Six Lessons

Such an experience inspired this book, which attempts to present John Paul's most important teachings in *Salvifici Doloris*. In the apostolic letter, the pope shares a wealth of spiritual wisdom that I believe can bring knowledge, healing, and peace for those seeking meaning in suffering. While I highly recommend reading *Salvifici Doloris* in its entirety, I have also come to realize from my discussions with others that some of the material can be difficult to follow for the layperson without formal theological training. So, within these pages, I have tried to respond by distilling the pope's essential points from *Salvifici Doloris* and explaining them in six lessons that readers can easily remember and apply. Each lesson contains a pastoral discussion of key themes in *Salvifici Doloris*; at the same time, I have also incorporated passages from Scripture, thoughts from other great writers and saints, and my own stories and reflections, in hope that this approach enriches a reader's appreciation and understanding of John Paul's teaching.

In an ideal world where time and word count were not factors, I could have included lessons drawn from the pope's entire corpus of public addresses and writings pertaining to human suffering. But such a work would have required many years and volumes to produce. By contrast, my purpose for this book is to provide a relatively short and useful spiritual "companion" to illuminate the pope's teaching about the Christian meaning of suffering. Although the majority of the book's material stems from *Salvifici Doloris*, I have taken the liberty to quote from John Paul's other writings at times when they are particularly relevant. The most important of these is a collection of the pope's prayers and public teachings on suffering in the book *The Loving Heart: The Private Prayers of Pope John Paul II* (New York: Atria Books, 2005).

From the outset, I also want to state that although this book welcomes all readers regardless of their religious backgrounds, it is written from a distinctively Roman Catholic perspective. Roman Catholicism was the Christian faith tradition of Pope John Paul II and is the one in which I have come to know God and to receive God's love and truth most fully. In the following pages, I have tried to engage in an honest discussion of the tough questions about the problem of suffering, many of which are common to Christians as well as non-Christians, but I have done so in a spirit of humble fidelity to the teachings of the Roman Catholic Church as they have been presented by the pope.

And so we begin our exploration of the Christian meaning of suffering with Pope John Paul as our guide. Scarcely could we ever find a better spiritual leader for such a pilgrimage. Esteemed as one of the most brilliant and beloved religious figures of the modern era, John Paul was an apostle of hope to sufferers throughout his life, and especially during his pontificate. Those who hurt both physically and spiritually found a special place in the pope's heart throughout his ministry, and it is to them that he gave his famous first words as Supreme Pontiff: "Be not afraid!"

John Paul's works of mercy, writings, and public addresses over his twenty-seven-year pontificate reveal his passionate desire to alleviate suffering by protecting human dignity and to comfort sufferers with the good news and love of our Lord.

A Man Familiar with Suffering

John Paul was especially sensitive to the human experience of suffering, for he also knew what it was like to suffer intensely. Death took young Karol Wojtyla's entire family from him by the time he was twenty, even as he struggled to stay alive while the Nazi regime brutalized his homeland of Poland. Alone after the loss of his loved ones, twenty-one-year-old Karol began backbreaking work in Poland's stone quarries to avoid being sent to labor camps in Germany and was hospitalized a couple of years later, after being hit by a military truck. Amid all this suffering, he decided to become a priest — an effort that proved to be an uphill battle, as Communist rule in Poland made it necessary for him to pursue his ordination by attending clandestine seminary classes hidden from the government's watchful eye.

Within the next two decades, Fr. Karol Wojtyla — known for his prayerful spirit, superb intellect, and charming personality — was appointed Auxiliary Bishop of Krakow, Archbishop of Krakow, and eventually, consecrated a Cardinal. In 1978, after the untimely death of Pope John Paul I, Cardinal Wojtyla ascended to the chair of St. Peter as Pope John Paul II.

It was during this time of papal ministry that the world became a firsthand witness to the pope's suffering. Three years into his pontificate, John Paul was shot and critically wounded by an assassin in Rome but recovered after emergency surgery. The pope narrowly dodged a second attempt on his life just a year later, when a man tried to stab him in Fatima, Portugal. But perhaps the most vivid memories of John Paul "the sufferer" come from his struggle to carry the heavy burdens of aging that marked his later years. A dynamic orator and active sportsman for most of his life, the pope came to experience slurred speech, the shaking of Parkinson's disease, and confinement to a wheelchair as he grew increasingly older. For those of us who had witnessed the earlier years of his career, it seemed like such a strange phenomenon to see this holy man, known for his strength, charisma, and vitality, grow weaker by the day.

But there, in the twilight of his life until his death in April 2005, John Paul taught his greatest lessons on suffering as he endured his own trials with faith, hope, love, courage, and dignity. He humbly persevered through great anguish to continue his life of prayer, to proclaim God's Word to the world, and to fulfill his many responsibilities as the earthly shepherd of Christ's flock. Often seen clinging to the crucifix, the pope found solidarity with our Lord in His suffering, which he believed could become an instrument of grace for himself and others through the saving power of the Cross. Clearly, the good news that he preached so passionately during his papal ministry — that suffering has received saving meaning in Christ — became for him a personal truth on which he stood unshakable as he suffered himself.

With God's promises lighting the way, John Paul crossed the threshold of hope and showed us in deed what he taught us with his eloquent words. It is to these words that we now turn as we explore the meaning of suffering, one of the greatest mysteries of faith. My hope and prayer is that these pages inspired by the pope's wisdom will offer both intellectual and spiritual nourishment for the journey.

LESSON 1

To Live Is to Suffer

A typical day for most of us includes some form of suffering: the frustration of being late again for work; that sickly feeling in your gut before the big presentation; the strain of bearing your daily responsibilities under physical or emotional pain; sadness in the wake of tragedy or loss. Regardless of the scenario and its intensity, suffering is no stranger to our everyday lives.

Without apology or explanation, suffering has made us victims many times over. It can turn our hallelujahs to doubts, our laughs to tears, and our routines to chaos. Perhaps we could even say that we live on this earth as survivors who continue to dress our wounds caused by suffering's repeated blows. Try as we might to avoid it, suffering often proves too big and powerful a force to stop, a reality about which sickness and death constantly remind us.

Sadly, suffering has an uncanny knack for finding us. The reason, according to Pope John Paul II, is that suffering is a condition of our membership in the human race. The pope writes that suffering is the "universal theme that accompanies man at every point on earth . . . it co-exists with him in the world."[2] It is "the daily bread of human beings, the permanent condition of life in every age."[3] In these words, John Paul reminds us that we can't escape suffering because to live is to suffer — a lesson that our many hurts and tears have come to teach us all too well.

Remembering Our Story

As we grow older and carry on the business of living, we become increasingly aware of the abundant suffering that exists all around us. It is an undeniable character in our human story. Flipping back through the book of history, we see suffering scribbled all over its pages. Sickness and war, hatred and oppression, poverty and death — all have been among us from the start of human life.

As Christians we read of the long history of suffering among our spiritual ancestry in the Bible, which John Paul calls "a great book about suffering."[4] Throughout our written record of God's saving word, suffering has posed a serious problem. Jump back to the beginning of our story. The Book of Genesis tells how our first parents, Adam and Eve, encountered suffering for the first time through the angst of temptation, the guilt of sin, and the agony of death. There in the Garden of Eden, suffering made its infamous entrance onto the stage of humanity. But that was just the start.

Suffering continued to show its ugly face in many other forms to the men and women of the Old Testament: Abel's murder by his resentful brother, Cain (Gen. 4:8); the jealous betrayal of Joseph by his older brothers (Gen. 37:20-28); Israel's toil and oppression in Egypt (Ex. 1:11-14); Job's agonizing quest to make sense of his torments (Job 3 ff.); King David's tears after the slaying of his son, Absalom (2 Sam. 19:1). Countless testimonies of trial and affliction have been handed down to us from our first fathers and mothers in faith, who grappled with suffering in their own lives so long ago.

Some of the Old Testament's most profound words capturing the human struggle to live in the mystery suffering come from the Psalms. In these poetic prayers, the Psalmist often writes in a spirit of lament and cries out to God for deliverance from his agony. Psalm 102, for instance, bears the title, "A prayer of one afflicted, when he is faint and pours out his complaint before the LORD." It reads:

> Hear my prayer, O LORD;
>> let my cry come to you!
> Do not hide your face from me
>> in the day of my distress!
> Incline your ear to me;
>> answer me speedily in the day when I call!
> For my days pass away like smoke,
>> and my bones burn like a furnace.
> My heart is struck down like grass, and withered;
>> I forget to eat my bread.
> Because of my loud groaning
>> my bones cleave to my flesh.
> I am like a vulture of the wilderness,
>> like an owl of the waste places;
> I lie awake,
>> I am like a lonely bird on the housetop.
> All the day my enemies taunt me,
>> those who deride me use my name for a curse.
> For I eat ashes like bread,
> and mingle tears with my drink,
>> because of your indignation and anger;
>> for you have taken me up and thrown me away.
> My days are like an evening shadow;
>> I wither away like grass.
> But you, O LORD, are enthroned for ever;
>> your name endures to all generations.

— Ps. 102:1-12

Here, the Psalmist gives voice to feelings we all share at various times in our lives when things aren't going right. Bearing the weight of a great burden, he hears only God's silence and feels alone in his pain. Weakness plagues his body and spirit, as he comes to the realization that the days of his life are numbered. And, in his moment of distress, he begs God for help.

Flipping ahead in the pages of our spiritual story, we also see an abundance of suffering in the New Testament. Like the Old Testament, which begins with the sorrows of suffering accompanying the joyful event of God's new creation, the New Testament follows a similar trend.

The Gospel of Matthew tells us that horrific suffering accompanied the joyous birth of the Messiah, the one who would save God's people. Upon learning of the ancient prophecy that a new king of the Jews (Jesus) was to be born, King Herod orchestrated a wicked plot to have the newborn Messiah killed. Enraged when his plan failed, Herod massacred all of the baby boys in Bethlehem in an effort to protect his throne. How ironic that the jubilant birth of our Savior brought with it the "wailing and loud lamentation" of parents whose tiny sons were murdered by Herod's orders in Bethlehem (Mt. 2:16-18).

At the same time, much of the New Testament describes Jesus' public ministry, in which our Lord found himself immersed in a community of sufferers who hurt and looked to Him for healing. Read a few pages of any of the Gospels, and it's clear that a typical day for Jesus involved ministering to people like the blind Bartimaeus, who lived in darkness (Mk. 10:46-52), the centurion who mourned his servant's terminal illness (Mt. 8:5-13), and the woman ravaged by hemorrhages (Mk. 5:25-34). Such accounts inform us that Jesus dedicated a large part of His life to comforting those around Him who were in pain. He felt especially drawn to the sufferers of His time and worked to bring them spiritual and physical healing.

Based on the biblical memories of Jesus' life, we see that He could empathize with those who hurt because He also knew what it was like to suffer. He shed tears at the death of His friend, Lazarus (Jn. 11:35), and fought temptation during His forty-day retreat in the desert after His baptism (Lk. 4:1-13). In Jesus' final days, the passion narratives tell us how He felt the heartbreak of being betrayed by a good friend, the humiliation of public persecution for His beliefs, and the excruciating pain of being tortured to death — a cup from which the apostles would also drink as the consequence of their faith.

Today, thousands of years after Scripture's writing, suffering still plagues our story. All of creation groans in travail (Rom. 8:22), as St. Paul observed. Even if our own anguish didn't constantly remind us of our suffering world, the modern media make it impossible to forget. Just click on one of the cable news networks, tune into the radio, surf the Internet, or read the newspaper, and a barrage of reports explain in painstaking detail how suffering blankets our planet.

On Friday nights, after the long work week is over and our baby daughter, Elizabeth, is fast asleep, Sarah and I usually make microwaveable dinners and relax in front of the TV while we eat. Our little dinner date over soggy pizza and cardboard-flavored veggies usually coincides with the evening news, which slings headlines of widespread starvation, genocide, war, terrorism, abortion, poverty, murder, and other evils taking the world by storm. As Sarah and I listen to the massive suffering reported, we can't help but react: "Oh, no!" "That's terrible!" "How could that happen?" "God help them!" It's all so depressing that, after just a few minutes, we usually end up popping in a movie to try to escape our feelings of sadness about what we've seen. The reality of suffering is just too hard to face.

Nevertheless, the abundance and diversity of human pain reported by the media only remind us of what we already know from our own experience. Suffering is a fundamental and unavoidable part of our earthly lives. In the words of John Paul, "suffering seems to be, and is, almost *inseparable from man's earthly existence.*"⁵ Perhaps this is the most formidable challenge of living — contending with the truth that suffering is, and will be, a part of our story. Along with any happiness or peace we may come to know in this life, trial and tribulation will also form the context of our earthly existence.

Sinful Roots

According to the Book of Genesis, Satan and human sin are to blame for the sad fact of suffering. Chapter 3 describes a disruption in creation, when Adam and Eve abused their freedom by giving in to the serpent (Satan)'s coaxing to rebel against God. Because of their disobedience, pain and suffering multiplied on earth. And the harmony that had once existed between human beings, God, and creation fell apart.

Reading through the creation story, we see that suffering was not part of God's original blueprint for the world. Pain and death came to exist not by God's will but through the tangled mess of human sin. John Paul explains, "suffering cannot be divorced from the sins of the beginnings, from what St. John calls 'the sin of the world' (Jn. 1:29)."⁶ Reflecting on Genesis, the pope affirms the longstanding belief in the Judeo-Christian tradition that suffering is not of God but is of man and woman.

As Christians, we see this connection between suffering and the sin of humanity through the lens of original sin, which has a twofold meaning. In one sense, original sin refers to a historical event described in Genesis — that first personal act of human disobedience which offended God, subjected creation to suffering, and introduced sin and death into the world (cf. Rom. 5:19; 8:20). But original sin also points to a spiritual disorder of our human nature — the condition of weakness within us that blinds us to truth and attracts us to evil over good.

A quick look at the world around us makes it clear that in both its historical and spiritual dimensions, original sin has produced effects that we continue to bear. After all, none of us can entirely escape the prospect of pain and death, or the allure of sin in our lives.

On January 6, 2006, Sarah and I experienced the joy of welcoming our beautiful daughter, Elizabeth, to our family. Even though she weighed a healthy eight pounds when she was born, I remember how afraid I was to dress Elizabeth and change her diaper when she was a newborn. She was so tiny and delicate — I feared that I might unintentionally hurt her as I maneuvered her little arms and legs into position.

Thinking back to Elizabeth's first days of life — and, now, watching her develop as a toddler — I find it hard to believe that she could be stained by any kind of sin. Sure, she has a knack for making poopy diapers right in the middle of our dinner, and for waking us at all hours of the night for a feeding. But these acts, which cause us a little suffering, are certainly not intentional or malicious on Elizabeth's part. At this stage of her life, she's incapable of making a sinful choice. Her budding intellect will take another six years to reach the age of reason, and her physical capabilities, while expanding rapidly, are still very limited. And yet the Christian tradition teaches that Elizabeth has inherited original sin.

Obviously, she has not freely chosen to violate God's law and isn't culpable of personal sin. But as a human person, Elizabeth shares in the condition of what St. Thomas Aquinas calls the sin of the human race. Like all of us, she must suffer anguish at the hands of this world and will someday take up spiritual arms for her battle with sin. Forced to endure these afflictions inherent to our created world, she and the rest of us stand as a people scourged by what has become known as Adam's Fall.

Such is the conviction expressed in John Milton's seventeenth-century Christian epic, *Paradise Lost*. Having written the work in his retirement after he had gone blind, Milton reflects on the origins of evil according to the Genesis creation account. At the end of the poem, Michael the Archangel shows Adam the terrible consequences of his Fall in a dream.

In his first vision, Adam sees the innocent death of his son, Abel — brutally murdered by his brother, Cain. Horrified at the sight, Adam laments over Cain's malicious deed and Abel's appalling death. Adam realizes that both tragedies were effects of his own disobedience and becomes terrified at the prospect of tasting death himself:

> "Alas! Both for the deed, and for the cause!
> But have I now seen Death? Is this the way
> I must return to native dust? O sight
> Of terrour, foul and ugly to behold,
> Horrid to think, how horrible to feel!"[7]

Then Michael reveals to Adam, in painstaking detail, the entire world of suffering and its abundance of miseries. For the first time, Adam sees the innumerable paths that lead to death — fires, floods, famine, intemperance, and "all maladies of ghastly spasm, or racking torture, qualms of heart-sick agony, all feverish kinds."[8] Eyes burning with tears, Adam protests the anguish his progeny will be forced to bear during their lifetime. He questions the purpose of trying to go on living in a world where the promise of suffering is certain:

> "O miserable mankind, to what fall
> Degraded, to what wretched state reserved!
> Better end here unborn. Why is life giv'n
> To be thus wrested from us? rather, why

Obtruded on us thus? Who, if we knew
What we receive, would either not accept
Life offered, or soon beg to lay it down;
Glad to be so dismissed in peace."[9]

On some level, I think we can all relate to these despondent
words from Milton's Adam when suffering has pushed us to our
breaking point — that place of desperation where we're on the
brink of losing it and ready to jump. Sometimes the thought of
living through another day under the burden of suffering can
seem unbearable. In John Paul's words, "The mystery of pain
tortures our existence. It isn't easy to accept pain and death,
because it means accepting our frailty in its many forms."[10] Confronted by our own weakness in a world of pain that doesn't
add up, we long to be freed from the evil that surrounds us. And
in our moments of trial, we realize our need to be saved.

The good news of the Gospel is that Jesus Christ has
already come, offering salvation to all. St. Paul speaks of Jesus
as the new Adam, who, through faithful obedience to God,
reversed the harmful effects of Adam's sin. In his letter to the
Romans, Paul makes the case that where Adam's sin infected
the world with death, condemnation, and sinfulness, Jesus'
acceptance of the Father's will unto death provided the cure —
life, forgiveness, and righteousness (cf. Rom. 5:17-19).

But if Jesus righted Adam's wrongs that brought suffering
into the world, why do we still suffer? This is a great mystery. Yet
Jesus himself informed His disciples that the earth wouldn't
break free from the shackles of suffering until He comes again
in glory. Sin and death, He predicted, would continue in this
world until His return to establish God's everlasting reign at the
end of time:

"And you will hear of wars and rumors of wars; see that
you are not alarmed; for this must take place, but the end
is not yet. For nation will rise against nation, and kingdom
against kingdom, and there will be famines and earth-
quakes in various places: all this is but the beginning of the
sufferings. . . . But he who endures to the end will be saved."

— MT. 24:6-8, 13

It's no secret that Jesus was right. The world of suffering He
described still surrounds us two millennia later and challenges
us to heed His call to patient endurance. At the same time,
because we live in a suffering world, we must struggle against
the many forces of evil constantly working to inflict physical
and spiritual pain on us. In the words of the Second Vatican
Council:

A monumental struggle against the powers of darkness per-
vades the whole history of man. The battle was joined from
the very origins of the world and will continue until the
last day, as the Lord has attested (cf. Matt. 24:13; 13:24-30
and 36-43). Caught in this conflict, man is obliged to wres-
tle constantly if he is to cling to what is good . . ."[11]

Experiencing Evil

Wrestling with evil is what defines the human experience of
suffering. Suffering, according to John Paul, is an experience of
evil.[12] In other words, our personal encounter with evil in its
many forms evokes the response of suffering within us. In light
of this intricate relationship between suffering and evil, we have
to then ask the next logical question: "What is evil?"[13] "This
question," says the pope, "seems, in a certain sense, inseparable from the theme of suffering."[14]

John Paul teaches us that evil is the absence or distortion of good. St. Augustine Christianized this idea of evil back in the fourth century, and the pope explains it to us in more detail:

> Christianity proclaims the essential good of existence and the good of that which exists, acknowledges the goodness of the Creator and proclaims the good of creatures. Man suffers on account of evil, which is a certain lack, limitation or distortion of good . . . because of a good in which he does not share, from which in a certain sense he is cut off, or of which he has deprived himself.[15]

Unlike other worldviews and religions that think of the world or human existence as something inherently evil, Christians believe God created a good world that is tainted by evil. Because creation is essentially good, evil can only occur where good is lacking. The presence of evil in the world is kind of like the holes in a piece of Swiss cheese. It is a negative reality that takes away from the good and whole order of God's creation.

Whenever I try to understand this concept of evil, I think about my eyes. Many years ago when I was a sixth-grader at Our Lady of Lourdes grade school, I remember going to the school nurse's office for the annual student eye exam. After attempting to read the fuzzy little letters on the chart, I heard the words that no ten-year-old boy wants to hear: "Rob, you need glasses."

Stricken by the prospect of being called "four eyes," I panicked. "Are you sure?" I asked the nurse in disbelief. Then I began to wonder. *How will I be able to play basketball, and baseball, and soccer with glasses on my face? Will the other kids think I look goofy?*

Once I broke the news to my mom, she whisked me away to the eye doctor, who confirmed that I had astigmatism and required glasses. But he also found another, more serious problem. I suffered from glaucoma, a disease of the optic nerve that can cause blindness. It results when there is too much fluid inside the eye and causes pressure to build up. When the pressure gets too high, permanent vision loss can occur. Fortunately for me, the glaucoma hadn't caused any damage to my eyes. But in order to keep them healthy, I would have to take medicated eye drops for the rest of my life.

Twenty years later, wearing my contact lenses and taking eye medication for my glaucoma are as second nature as breathing. However, both of these habits compensate for "goods" of the eye that I possess in only a limited or distorted way — namely, sight and normal eye pressure. Evil, as the pope has taught us, is present in the gaps where these goods are absent.

So suffering is "experienced evil" that deprives us of the good we were meant to have as human persons. And this experience is one of the whole person, composed of both a body and a soul — the two essential dimensions of our being. According to John Paul, we suffer both bodily and spiritually in accord with who we are as persons; suffering results when we lack the good we were meant to have in one of these two aspects of our selfhood.[16]

Bodily suffering is probably the most obvious kind of experienced evil that we face. From the time we get our first cold or skinned knee as children, we learn that our bodies are vulnerable and that the physical structure that gives form to us is far from invincible. Sometimes, forces both inside and outside of the body overpower it and cause it to hurt or break down. Whether it thrusts itself upon us suddenly or creeps into our flesh over a long period of time, bodily suffering takes many unmistakable shapes and sizes — broken bones, stuffy noses, headaches, heart disease, cancer, labor pains, indigestion, and countless other distresses.

One of the hallmarks of bodily suffering is the physical pain or discomfort it causes us to feel. Burns, pierces, aches, and throbs permeate our bodies and force us to endure these uncomfortable, sometimes miserable, sensations that alert us to something physically wrong. Bearing these bodily pains, as we have all come to know, is tiring, frustrating, and depressing. And the more our bodies suffer, the more we understand where Job was coming from when he said, "Days of affliction have taken hold of me. The night racks my bones, and the pain that gnaws me takes no rest" (Job 30:16-17).

St. Bernadette Soubirous, who received apparitions of the Virgin Mary in Lourdes France during the mid-nineteenth century, certainly knew the meaning of these words. From the time she entered the convent at age twenty-two until her death thirteen years later, she suffered from asthma and tuberculosis. A priest who frequently visited Bernadette recalls her intense bodily suffering:

> Chronic asthma, chest pains, accompanied by spitting up of blood, went on for two years. An aneurysm, gastralgia, and a tumor of the knee developed. Finally, during the last few years she suffered from bone decay, so that her poor body was the vessel of all kinds of pain and suffering.[17]

Toward the end of her life, when her bodily afflictions were the most severe, St. Bernadette remarked, "I have been ground in the mill like a grain of wheat. I would never have thought that one must suffer so much to die."[18]

While bodily suffering is typically synonymous with the sensation of pain, there are also situations when our bodies suffer immensely without feeling a lot of physical discomfort.

One night some years ago, my father was playing in a softball game on a steamy July evening. As the game went on, however, he noticed something strange — he wasn't perspiring. Over the next couple of days, he still couldn't break a sweat, so he went to the doctor. Tests confirmed that the cause of his problem was a nine-pound cancerous tumor that had been growing for months inside his colon. Surprisingly, Dad was completely oblivious that it was even there. He had felt nothing.

Reflecting on this situation, I can't help but think how ironic it is that a minor ailment like a headache or tooth cavity would have caused Dad more bodily pain than the malignant and deadly tumor that grew silently inside his body. Eventually, the removal of that tumor and the spread of cancer brought him horrible pain, but at its onset the disease was like a ghost to him. So it seems that bodily suffering isn't necessarily limited to the experience of pain alone. Sometimes, our bodies can also suffer in silence.

As I recall my dad's story, it occurs to me that one of the most formidable challenges of coping with physical suffering is living in the mystery of the body's openness to restoration. We all know that sometimes the body can be healed and sometimes it can't. In most cases, our ability to recover depends not only on the strength of our organs and immune system but the type of ailment that afflicts us and the treatments available.

Think back to your last cold. Probably within a week after your cough and stuffiness started, they went away, and you were back to your old self again. Perhaps your body was entirely self-healing and conquered the germs that attacked it by its own power. Or maybe your body recovered by cooperating with the chemicals in medicines or with alternative therapies because it didn't possess sufficient resources to heal itself. Regardless, anyone who has ever bounced back from an ailment or injury knows firsthand how amazing the body's ability to heal really is.

But we also know that some kinds of bodily suffering are more complicated and can't be healed. They prove insurmountable as the body appears completely closed to recovery and rejects the help of even the most advanced remedies. In such cases, we face the daunting and heartbreaking task of enduring our afflictions with little or no hope of getting better, and with full knowledge that death is near. Indeed, the inherent weakness of our bodies throughout the course of our lives serves as a herald of our mortality — a constant reminder of that future moment which awaits us all, when we will breathe our last and leave this world in death.

While we tend to associate most of the hurt we feel with bodily suffering, John Paul reminds us that human suffering is even wider and more complex than physical illness or pain.[19] We also experience spiritual or moral suffering, which the pope calls "pain of the soul."[20]

Spiritual suffering is an interior affliction, as opposed to bodily suffering, which attacks our physical selves. It involves struggles of the soul such as guilt from sin, dryness in prayer, or feeling distant from God. Spiritual suffering also includes forms of psychological and emotional distress such as disappointment, discouragement, frustration, depression, anxiety, sadness, or despair. According to John Paul:

> The vastness and the many forms of moral suffering are certainly no less in number than the forms of physical suffering. But at the same time, moral suffering seems as it were less identified and less reachable by therapy.[21]

Spiritual or moral suffering, while as prevalent in our lives as bodily suffering, tends to be more difficult to put under the microscope and fix. As an inner reality, it is often felt but not seen.

Within the Christian tradition, spiritual suffering is a perennial theme in the writings of the saints. In *Dark Night of the Soul,* Spanish poet and mystic St. John of the Cross describes in exquisite detail the pain of the dark night in which the soul feels abandoned by God. In this place of darkness, prayer feels impossible. And even when the soul does try to pray, St. John writes, "It does so with such lack of strength and of sweetness that it thinks that God neither hears it nor pays heed to it."[22] Like Jeremiah, who thought that God set a cloud in his prayer's path as an obstacle, one who lives in the shadows of the dark night echoes the prophet's words: "Though I call and cry for help, he shuts out my prayer."[23]

In the twentieth century, Polish nun and mystic St. Faustina wrote in her diary about a similar experience of spiritual suffering that she called the "terror of the soul." She found herself in a state of torture when she couldn't find words for prayer and felt separated from God. Here is how she describes her suffering:

> The soul is engulfed in a horrible night. It sees within itself only sin. It feels terrible. It sees itself completely abandoned by God. It feels itself to be the object of His hatred . . . It raises its eyes to heaven, but is convinced that this is not for her — for her all is lost. It falls deeper and deeper from darkness to darkness, and it seems to it that it has lost forever the God it used to love so dearly. This thought is torture beyond all description.[24]

Both St. John of the Cross and St. Faustina were mystics who experienced God's presence in ways most of us only dream about. Perhaps even the most contemplative among us can't fully empathize with their words of spiritual pain. But I think all of us have shared similar kinds of spiritual suffering. We too know what it's like to struggle with prayer, to call upon faith only to find doubt, and to feel like God has forgotten about us. Such is a typical day in the life of a believer, seeking to serve and love an invisible and transcendent God whose ways we can't always figure out. Our encounters with evil not only wound our bodies but also pain our souls. Indeed, suffering penetrates us to the core.

Recently my dog, Prinnie, and I were out for a routine stroll through the neighborhood on a chilly October afternoon. Along the way my neighbor, Tim, flagged us down.

"How's the baby?" he asked, with a grin.

"Doing great, getting big!" I replied.

As the conversation progressed, Tim's smile began to fade. He paused for a few seconds. "You know I've been out of work," he said. "I had a stroke a couple months ago, and when I went into the hospital to get checked out, they also found heart problems. I need to have surgery in a couple weeks to clean out my arteries."

I couldn't believe it. Tim lived an active lifestyle and was always busy in his yard. He wasn't the kind of person I would have expected to develop heart problems.

"How are you handling all of this? Are you okay?" I asked.

"I can't do much anymore because I get tired so quickly," Tim said with a sigh. "I'm not nervous about the surgery now, but I'm sure I will be. I just really miss going to work. I just can't wait to get back."

Tim's suffering body had taken him in a direction he didn't want to go. In addition to his fear of the surgery and the many risks involved, Tim felt isolated and longed to get back in the groove of his regular work routine. But he would have to wait and see how the surgery turned out. His future was uncertain, and he was afraid.

For Tim and all of us, bodily suffering and spiritual suffering don't exist in isolation. Like two dominoes, when one falls, it causes the other to topple; when the body hurts, the spirit hurts, and vice versa. The reason for this correlation between bodily and spiritual suffering, says John Paul, is that the human person is a *psychological and physical "whole."*[25] Fr. Jim Willig bears witness to this truth in *Lessons from the School of Suffering,* an inspiring testimony of his long and arduous bout with cancer. He writes:

> Early on in my struggles with cancer, I was caught up with many of the fears and anxieties that go hand in hand with cancer. I would be so tempted to think, "Renal cell cancer, once it [is] metastasized, is rarely curable." As long as I had to look at that fact, I felt myself slowly sinking into a type of depression. There were so many questions that become distractions. "What about this treatment?" "What about that clinic?" "How about this medicine or chemotherapy?"
>
> I became so overwhelmed that I started to feel like I was actually losing my equilibrium. I thought I was going crazy. I cried out to God, "Lord, I am afraid I'm going to lose it. You've got to help me, Lord. I'm sinking here."[26]

Fr. Jim's honest words describe the nature of suffering as an affliction of the whole person. Bodily suffering doesn't stay contained in flesh and blood. It seeps into the pores of our being and begins producing interior side effects. In the case of Fr. Jim, cancer penetrated beyond the physical realm to spawn unwelcome fears and spiritual unrest.

Conversely, spiritual suffering often causes distress within the body. According to John Paul, sufferings of the spirit "have a 'physical' or somatic element, and . . . are often reflected in the state of the entire organism."[27] The pope directs our attention especially to the writings of the Old Testament, which frequently expresses spiritual suffering by using words that relate to the body.[28] For instance, King Hezekiah felt forsaken by God when sickness left him standing on the precipice of death and wrote: "I cry for help until morning; like a lion he breaks all my bones" (Is. 38:13). Job also expressed his spiritual brokenness in bodily terms as he suffered from disease and the grief of losing his children to death: "He [God] seized me by the neck and dashed me to pieces . . . he slashes open my kidneys, and does not spare; he pours out my gall on the ground" (Job 16:12-13).

One obvious example of how this body-spirit link plays out today is the impact our hyper-stressed lifestyles are having on our physical health. In *Peace of Soul,* Archbishop Fulton Sheen writes of the excessive psychological and emotional forms of spiritual suffering that exist in contemporary society:

> An increasing number of persons are afflicted with neuroses, complexes, fears, irritabilities, and ulcers; they are, perhaps, not so much "run down" as "wound up"; not so much set on fire by the sparks of daily life as they are burning up from internal combustion.[29]

While it's true that a limited amount of anxiety gives us the healthy boost of adrenaline we need to meet the challenges of life, we have a tendency nowadays to overdose. Medical research has proven that too much stress contributes to the six leading causes of death — heart disease, cancer, lung ailments, accidents, liver disease, and suicide.

So just as physical suffering permeates our inner self, internal suffering rises to the surface of our bodies. Our experience of suffering affects us both from the inside out and the outside in. Suffering in both its physical and spiritual dimensions, says John Paul, "is undoubtedly one of the most moving mysteries of existence, for it touches each of us closely, excluding none."[30] Indeed, suffering is the way we experience evil, which saps the good God created us to have as human persons.

Knowing Our Limitations

When we suffer bodily and spiritually, we enter into a new reality that contrasts with our normal way of life. We cross over the threshold from how life was without suffering to how life is with suffering. Suffering disrupts our spiritual and physical equilibrium, arrests our concentration, and limits our activities. In the pope's words, suffering is "a 'limitation' and an 'ordeal' . . . a stumbling block on the road of life."[31] It prevents a father from giving his daughter a piggyback ride, a teenager from dancing at the prom, a mother from tending her garden, or a grandfather from going to his grandson's baseball games. It makes the brilliant student distracted in class, the diligent employee lax on the job, and the believer a skeptic in prayer. Indeed, suffering has a way of imposing its own set of rules for our lives.

Suffering has always had the upper hand in our created world, to the extent that we don't have the power to completely avoid it. However, our capabilities to lessen human hurt have changed significantly with the times. If you turn back the clock a couple hundred years, suffering would have probably looked much fiercer than it does today, because of certain limitations of knowledge and technology during that era.

Imagine you've been transported back to the nineteenth century. Feeling the sun warm your shoulders on a picture-perfect spring afternoon, you start to saddle up your horse for a ride into town. But suddenly, a piercing pain strikes your lower abdomen. After a few moments pass you think you know what the problem is — it's just indigestion from all those beans you ate for lunch. As the pain intensifies though, you begin to worry and decide to walk back to your house and rest. Step by step you hurt worse, but eventually you make it back inside. You take a couple shots of whiskey to help numb the pain, and then lie down. But within a few hours, you're burning up with fever and sick with nausea as your gut feels like it's about to explode.

Assuming you've brought your knowledge of the twenty-first century back in time, you realize your symptoms are hallmarks of appendicitis, an inflammation of the appendix, which must be surgically removed before it ruptures. You reach for the telephone to call 911, but then you remember — it hasn't been invented yet! Nor have the drugs or medical procedures that would help ease your pain. At this time in history, no one really knows what appendicitis is or how to treat it. And even if surgery was an option, you would have to go under the knife without anesthesia, because it, too, hasn't been discovered.

But you're tough. You decide you can handle the pain — it's a life or death decision, right? You'll find a surgeon who will operate on you and just take your chances. The only wrinkle in your plan is that even if all goes well with the surgery, preventing infection from setting in afterwards will be a problem. Penicillin and other antibiotic drugs that ward off infections didn't exist until the early twentieth century. Tragically, the prognosis for you and others facing severe cases of appendicitis at this time in history is bleak — widespread infection throughout the body, severe pain, and finally death.

Contrast that scenario of suffering with what would happen today if you contracted the exact same condition. Once you suspected you were suffering from a serious problem, you would grab your phone and call 911. An ambulance would whisk you off to your local hospital equipped with an arsenal of competent surgeons, computerized machines to pinpoint your problem, painkilling medications to help you relax, and IV antibiotics to ensure that your infection heals properly. You could potentially check in, have the surgery, and be back home resting, on your way to a full recovery — all in the same day.

Over the centuries, scientific research and technological advancements have helped reduce our suffering significantly. Just last week, we took a family trip to the pediatrician's office in order to have Elizabeth vaccinated against several diseases that could threaten her health. The method that protects our precious baby girl and millions of others goes back to 1796, when Edward Jenner found out that if he injected dead bacteria or toxins into people, he could protect them against more serious illnesses like smallpox in his own day. After Jenner, we won many more battles on the suffering front with the discovery of anesthesia and its power over pain, the X-ray's diagnostic capabilities, penicillin's potency to fight infection, and DNA's instructions for how the body works. Today, we stand on the shoulders of these landmarks in human ingenuity, which continue to proliferate in an effort to mitigate human pain.

And yet, despite such triumphs of our collective intelligence and creativity, John Paul reminds us that human power over pain has limits.[32] This truth becomes crystal clear when I visit the grave of my son, Bobby, who was strangled by his umbilical cord in the womb only five months after he was conceived; when I drive by the wooden cross nailed to a telephone pole that marks the spot where the body of my friend, Pete, was shattered in a car crash; when I remember those men, women, and children who go to bed each night not knowing whether they will live to see tomorrow because they are starving; when I think about the millions of innocent babies who never saw the light of day because they were massacred by abortion doctors. Then I remember the magnitude of suffering and how helpless we often become in its grasp.

Researchers in the field of medicine will even admit that suffering puts us on the defensive. It is impossible to prevent and eliminate all diseases, mainly because bacteria become resistant to antibiotics and then mutate to create new infections. As medical treatments become successful at treating one kind of sickness, new challenges emerge down the road and force us to go back to the drawing board to find cures.

But even if we did have a prescription for every physical manifestation of suffering, we would still suffer the consequences of being imperfect creatures living in an imperfect world. We would still feel lonely when we crave love, guilty when we sin, sad when we've been hurt, or frustrated when life isn't what we want it to be. Likewise, our ignorance and bad decisions would continue to produce consequences that goof things up and create pain for ourselves and others.

Such is the reality of living in a world of suffering. While we continue to develop our capabilities to lessen our hurt in many ways, those capabilities will never become so advanced as to eliminate suffering as a condition of our existence. As much as we like to be in the driver's seat controlling what happens in our lives, suffering typically turns the tables on us. It forces us to accept the fact that we can't control everything. Indeed, nothing reminds us of this truth more than suffering.

The reason, according to John Paul, is that suffering by nature is a passive experience. Suffering possesses what the pope calls a "passive character"[33] because it is an experience of evil that evokes a response of pain or distress within us that is beyond our complete control. Suffering is something that happens to us, versus something we do. In the words of the pope, "Even when man brings suffering on himself, when he is its cause, this suffering remains something passive."[34]

While suffering as an experience essentially victimizes us, it's clear that we do have some control over the circumstances that cause us to suffer. As John Paul has pointed out, some of our trials result from the exercise of human freedom when we or others make bad decisions and mistakes. With few exceptions, persecution, war, crime, and poverty demonstrate types of suffering for which human beings stand personally or collectively responsible. Such large-scale evils find their roots in human soil fertilized by hatred, anger, revenge, greed, ignorance, ambition, and confusion. But human-made suffering also comes in smaller packages — the broken ankle from wearing dress shoes in the snow, the overdraft charges from a math error in the check book, the nausea from failing to check the expiration date on the milk carton.

At the same time, suffering can also be the consequence of our blind collision with situations and forces completely outside of any human control. We can think of examples such as miscarriages, stillbirths, mental illness, sickness in children, and hereditary diseases — occurrences of "senseless" suffering that usually fall outside the circle of human agency. Sometimes we can locate the sources of such afflictions in biology or genetics, while in other cases they just happen to us without a trace of evidence as to how or why. Regardless, it seems that this kind of suffering, over which we have no control or explanation, could only occur in a created world gone haywire.

A good deal of suffering, however, falls somewhere between the pain produced by human hands and senseless suffering over which we have no power. Take illness. Whether or not I get heart disease depends partially on the genetic inheritance I have received from my family, whom I love but didn't choose. I don't have a say over who my parents, grandparents, and great-grandparents are, or the physical characteristics I inherited from them. But my own personal decisions to exercise regularly, limit my intake of Big Macs and Whoppers, and steer clear of cigarette smoke, also play a big role in keeping my heart healthy. Whether or not my heart will remain strong or weaken depends on a mixture of factors within and outside of my own personal control.

The same principle can also be applied on a much larger scale. A number of environmental scientists are challenging the world community to be attentive to degrees of global warming and rising ocean temperatures that can fuel more severe hurricanes. In the 1970s, twenty percent of all hurricanes reached the most deadly level, category 4 or 5, where wind speeds exceed 131 miles per hour; by the 1990s, thirty-five percent of hurricanes reached category 4 or 5. Although both severity of hurricanes and global temperature changes cannot be attributed solely to human causes, we still need to be aware of our need to be careful stewards of the earth, to minimize potential tragedy or suffering that destructive habits may cause.

Often, the line between the suffering we have a hand in versus the suffering that "just happens to us" looks blurry. We can't always be sure what or who brings suffering into our lives. Sometimes, all we can know for sure is that we hurt. Nevertheless, suffering teaches us the unsettling truth that we don't have total control over things. We don't want to suffer, but we do anyway — a reality which confirms that as beings who are by nature "created," we don't get to choose the essential conditions of the world into which we're born. If it were up to us, suffering would cease to exist. And yet suffering continues, because it is the human condition. So the challenge of coping with the many limitations suffering imposes on us becomes ours by virtue of our existence.

A Suffering World

According to John Paul, we can think of suffering as its own world that co-exists within our own. He writes, "human suffering constitutes as it were a specific 'world' which exists together with man."[35] Here, the pope uses this term "world" to describe the total being or existence of human suffering. In other words, if you were to piece together the hurt felt by every human being, it would form a composite which is the world of suffering. So a small part of this world exists within each one of us in such a way that it sometimes appears in us and then moves on, while in other instances it "becomes deeply rooted" in us and abides for longer periods of time.[36]

Penetrating deeper into this reality of the world of suffering, the pope ascribes to it both personal and collective meanings. First and foremost, suffering is a very personal experience, in the sense that we suffer as individuals. The pope writes that suffering is "a finite and unrepeatable entity."[37] The hurt that each one of us feels is unique, even though it might be similar to the suffering of others around us. We're worried about our son failing English class, stressed about not having enough money in the checking account to cover another car repair, saddened by the hurtful words of our spouse, frustrated by chronic illness, or grieving over the death of someone we love.

In these and many other instances of suffering, the pope explains that our first response is "I am affected by . . . I experience a feeling, I suffer."[38] Then, we begin to ask, "Why me?" or "How can I bear this?" We may even ask, "Is my life worth living?" Suffering moves from being an objective form of evil out there in the distance to something as personal as our own name. And, while we can find support and help from others, no one else can bear the suffering that belongs to us.

At the same time, suffering has a social dimension and is a common denominator of human existence. We all experience pain, and in that shared experience, we find solidarity with each other. The pope explains:

People who suffer become similar to one another through the analogy of their situation, the trial of their destiny, or through their need for understanding and care, and perhaps above all through the persistent question of the meaning of suffering.[39]

All of us are different in so many ways — our traditions, values, and preferences are as distinct and numerous as the stars in the universe. Yet suffering is an experience that every person on earth can relate to in one way or another. As a result, we're able to find comfort in the company of others who have walked in our shoes and know what we're going through. Although we ultimately must endure our suffering alone, we can transcend that isolation to some degree in realizing that others have shared similar experiences.

As we reflect on suffering in both its personal and social dimensions, John Paul calls our attention to how frequently it contracts and expands in size.[40] Sometimes suffering is miniscule. If I have a headache that a couple aspirin will remedy, the temporary pain I feel in my head could seem like a big deal. But it appears as a speck on the map of human suffering when compared to experiences where anguish is heavily concentrated — writhing in pain en route to the emergency room; getting diagnosed with a serious illness; receiving the news that a loved one has died unexpectedly; getting fired from your job; facing the devastation of natural disaster, praying for faith but unable to believe. In the blink of an eye, suffering can become a giant.

John Paul writes that the world of suffering has grown especially large in our present epoch in history. According to the pope, today we live in a "special world" of suffering that is particularly severe because of the massive amount of pain we as a collective people have brought on ourselves.[41] It is "a world which as never before has been transformed by progress through man's work, and at the same time, is as never before in danger because of man's mistakes and offences."[42]

Looking back on the events of the last century, I want to hold on tight to the first part of John Paul's comment — progress. There were so many firsts in a diversity of areas that almost every human activity became transformed. Think about it. The 1900s began with people getting from here to there by horses, and today we're zooming around in automobiles. Steam-powered ships were the most sophisticated means of transport, and now we overnight our packages on jets. Diseases that used to kill are now cured within a matter of days. And where the world of information was once available only in books, it's now stored digitally and accessible across the globe to anyone with a computer. The list of advancements is long and a source of great encouragement.

But along with all of our progress came suffering beyond compare. At the start of the twentieth century, we lived during the calm before the storm. We had not yet seen the 70 million killed and 55 million wounded in two World Wars, nor the millions of lives claimed in wars that followed. We didn't know about the ovens, gas chambers, and death camps that tortured and murdered 6 million Jewish men, women, and children; nor did we envision similar genocidal atrocities like the ones in Bosnia, Rwanda, and Darfur. We would have never have suspected that killing unborn babies by tearing them to pieces in the womb would become a societal norm. We didn't anticipate the massive devastation of terrorism. And we were oblivious to the frightening realities of nuclear warfare that threatens to exterminate the human race.

Today, as we stand in the dark shadow of these and many other gruesome events that mark our recent history, the pope writes that we experience "a much greater harvest of death and a much heavier burden of human sufferings."[43] He continues:

The second half of our century, in its turn, brings with it —
as though in proportion to the mistakes and transgressions
of our contemporary civilization — such a horrible threat
of nuclear war that we cannot think of this period in terms
of an incomparable accumulation of sufferings, even to the
possible self-destruction of humanity.[44]

It's hard to believe that we keep causing each other so much
pain. People just like you and me — with hopes and dreams,
spouses and children, brothers and sisters, mortgages and jobs
— have been, and continue to be, both agents of death and
helpless victims. Perhaps it is the differences of our hopes and
dreams, and the ways we intend to achieve them, that often
create conflict. Nevertheless, it's unfathomable how any differences, no matter how great, could lead to such a superabundance of bloodshed and suffering.

Perhaps such heartbreaking truths in our story reaffirm that
the presence of evil in our midst is undeniable. Even our happiest moments and most brilliant successes are often stained
by sin, ignorance, and pain. In those spaces where humanity is
not the cause of its own anguish, suffering still seems to find a
way in.

We open our eyes each day only to find ourselves alive in
a world of suffering which calls us to physical and spiritual battles — ones where anguish and pain leave us battered, bruised,
and in the shadow of death at the hands of these merciless
adversaries. And yet if we live rationally enlightened by faith,
we realize such combat, and any wounds we incur, are caused
by the forces of evil that inhabit the condition of our existence.
Indeed, as John Paul has taught us, to live is to suffer — a reality that each one of us must face head-on.

LESSON 2

God Expects Us to Ask "Why?"

When Sarah and I got married in 2003, we couldn't wait to have children. We often joked about how our lives would change once we had some little curly-headed monsters in dirty diapers running around the house. It was a beautiful vision for us — diapers and all. We passionately prayed that God would cooperate with us in creating life. And God answered in the affirmative.

Eight months into our marriage, we learned that Sarah was expecting. Any parent can relate to the pure exhilaration we felt. With our hearts bursting with joy, we took our parents and my grandparents out for a special dinner to thrill them with the good news that they would be grandparents and great-grandparents. Then the mass communication campaign began. We called and e-mailed all of our family and friends to let them know about our new little family member. It was a blessed time of celebration.

But six weeks into the pregnancy, Sarah started bleeding. After consulting with our doctor, we plummeted from joy to fear when we learned we might lose our baby. Sarah began taking some prescribed hormones to help our precious little one continue to grow properly, but there were no guarantees that they would work.

In the stressful days that followed, we pleaded with God to let our baby live. We expressed our love for our child to God and asked that we would have the chance to welcome our little one into the world. In the meantime, all of our loved ones assured us that they too were lifting up our baby in their prayers.

But on a February morning, prayers were not enough. We lost our baby to a miscarriage.

Many tears later, we decided to pick up the pieces of our hearts and try to have another child. Eight months after we said goodbye to our first child, whom we named Sam, we were thrilled to learn that Sarah was expecting again. This time though, the pregnancy looked perfect. There was no bleeding, the baby's heart was beating strong, and by the end of the first trimester, Sarah was toting a little round belly.

After losing our first child, we had recruited all of the prayer warriors we knew to ask God to protect our second baby. So our friends and family prayed and commissioned their friends and family to pray. All of the spiritual support we received was comforting. And the fact that the baby developed normally through the first trimester gave us a reserved confidence that all would go well.

When Sarah was five months along, it was time for another routine check-up at our doctor's office. As Sarah and I sat in the waiting room, we continued our ongoing debate over what the perfect name for our baby would be while we flipped through the latest issues of parenting magazines. We had agreed that if we had a boy, his name would be Robert George Schroeder, IV. Girl names were still up for grabs, with Elizabeth or Isabel being our favorites.

Before long, it was our turn in the examination room. We knew the drill. First, we would hear the baby's heart. Then the doctor would measure Sarah's uterus and tell us how the baby is growing.

While the nurse jellied up Sarah's belly to monitor the baby's heartbeat, we joked about past visits when it sounded like the drums of a marching band over the speaker. The nurse moved the instrument around Sarah's round mid-section, but we didn't hear anything. "Sometimes the baby is just hiding," the nurse said with a smile. This was no surprise to us. It had happened before.

But after a few minutes of moving the wand around, there was still silence. The nurse's relaxed hand tensed up and her smile disappeared. Sarah looked at me with fear in her eyes. A tear ran down her cheek. The nurse then called in the doctor, who used a different device to try to detect a heartbeat. Five minutes later, still nothing.

As Sarah began to weep, I'll never forget the doctor's words: "I'm concerned. It doesn't look good." A sonogram an hour later confirmed our worst nightmare — our beloved baby was dead.

Sarah, trembling, fell into my arms and sobbed. As I held her, I entered a dark fog, completely speechless. I felt a pain so deep it was as though the breath of life had been sucked out of me. We had been praying that God would protect our son. But now that we had lost two babies, God's silence to those prayers was deafening.

Because Sarah was well into her second trimester, delivery had to be induced at the hospital birthing center — the same place where we planned to deliver our baby four months later. We called our parents to break the terrible news to them, and then drove to the hospital. On the way, Sarah and I didn't speak. We just cried. And I remember thinking how life would never be the same for us. I wondered how we would go on living with so much pain.

After what seemed to be an eternity of a commute, we finally arrived at the hospital. As we walked to our room in the birthing center, the walls displayed pictures of newborns and other sentimental scenes depicting the beauty of new life and parenthood. I distinctly recall one that showed a father walking hand-in-hand with his little boy on the beach.

I held back tears thinking about the special times I might have shared with our child — snuggling over a warm bottle of milk, reading books together, teaching him or her to ride a bike, playing toss, taking the dog for long walks to the park, working on homework, attending sports games, coping with the awkwardness of adolescence, selecting the right college, watching him or her walk down the aisle, and one day becoming a grandparent. I realized that these dreams, so alive and vivid just a few hours earlier that day, had also died with our baby.

Once we arrived at the delivery room, more bad news followed. Our doctor warned us that Sarah's labor could last up to three days. She explained that because the baby was premature, Sarah's body wasn't ready to give birth and would likely be slow to release the baby — even with the help of inducing medications. I couldn't imagine Sarah suffering with the emotional and physical pain of trying to deliver our breathless baby for that long. I wanted so badly to pray for her, but how could I? I felt that God had abandoned us. But I managed to pull together some scraps of faith and asked God to hold her in his hands.

Twelve hours later at 8:15 a.m. on January 22, 2005, our son, Robert George Schroeder IV, was born. The nurse gave his tiny lifeless body to me, and I held Bobby for the first time. Motionless and underdeveloped, Bobby lay swaddled in a white delivery blanket with a little knit hat on his head. He was our beautiful boy. His umbilical cord, strung tightly around his neck, was the alleged cause of our little one's premature death.

As I cradled him in my arms, a thousand different emotions swept through my heart at once. I couldn't understand why this was happening to us. We were faithful Christians who sought to do God's will, and everyone had been praying for our baby.

"Why, God?" I cried. "Why our son? Why us?" I wanted answers but found only an abyss of silence.

The Universal Question

If suffering is the universal human condition, then "Why?" is the universal human question. We live in a world of suffering, but why is this so? Why do babies like Sam and Bobby have to suffer and die, and why must their parents face a lifetime of grief? For that matter, why does any one of us have to suffer and die in this life? And why do some among us suffer more severely than others?

Longing to ascribe some kind of purpose to our pain, we grapple with these mysterious questions. John Paul writes:

> Within each form of suffering endured by man, and at the same time at the basis of the whole world of suffering, there inevitably arises the question: why? It is a question about the cause, the reason, and equally, about the purpose of suffering . . . a question about its meaning.[45]

"Why?" is not a surprising question for us to ask because, as rational beings, we are meaning-makers. Hard-wired into us are both a deep desire and a need to make sense of the experiences that form our earthly lives. Our minds, powered by reason, drive us to seek answers and to draw conclusions by reflecting on ourselves and the world around us. We constantly strive to decode the mystery of our existence and to discover a central purpose to which we can dedicate ourselves.

The underlying assumption of our quest for answers, of course, is the belief that our lives, and the world stage on which they play out, are not completely chaotic and absurd. As disordered and crazy as things sometimes seem, we hold fast to the notion that there is some underlying order and meaning that we can come to know.

According to John Paul, this capacity for self-reflection and our will to find meaning uniquely characterize the human dimension of suffering. They differentiate our suffering from that of animals, which also live under the heavy burden of pain. The deer that lies shattered and bleeding on the roadside, after having been hit by a car, feels agonizing pain. However, the deer doesn't possess the rational faculties to seek any kind of understanding about the meaning of its anguish.

But put a human being in the same situation and you get a litany of why's and what-for's. Face-down on the pavement, limbs paralyzed, and writhing in pain, we become philosophers trying to make sense of our experience. We ask: "Why did this happen to me? What did I do to deserve this? Am I going to die? How can I go on living with this pain?" While suffering and pain also exist among animals, the pope writes that "only the suffering human being knows that he is suffering and wonders why; and he suffers in a humanly speaking still deeper way if he does not find a satisfactory answer."[46]

As the pope points out, we have the innate capacity and motivation to put our pain into context through interpretation. But when our afflictions don't make sense, we experience confusion and anxiety, which add a new psychological dimension to the suffering we already feel. It's the proverbial snowball effect. You take a small ball of snow and drop it at the top of a snow-covered hill. As the ball rolls down the slope, it will pick up more snow and keep increasing in size. In a similar way, our failure to understand why we hurt causes our world of suffering to grow larger.

The Road to Meaning

The road to meaning in suffering twists and turns through many peaks and valleys. At times we can find answers with confidence and accuracy, while in other circumstances we're left bewildered and speechless. Nevertheless, our ability to understand why we suffer hinges on how we frame the question.

As the pope has mentioned, one sense in which we seek meaning in suffering has to do with the cause or origin of our pain. We pose a basic cause-and-effect type of question that tries to pinpoint the source of our bodily or spiritual suffering. For instance, if you're experiencing chest pain, you want to know "Why?" in terms of what is causing the piercing sensation you're feeling. Are you having a heart attack or simply heartburn from the spicy chili you ate? Likewise, if you're depressed to the point where you no longer want to get out of bed in the morning, you want to know "Why?" in terms of what is causing you to despair. Are you dissatisfied with important aspects of your life, or do you need medical therapy to treat a chemical imbalance in your body? In such cases, asking why we suffer takes its place in the process of diagnosis, where we try to identify the cause of our pain so that we can apply the proper remedies to alleviate it.

The mere ability to understand why we hurt the way we do in this causal context often brings a sense of peace, even if we can't be entirely cured. Putting our finger on the source of our pain gives us at least some rational explanation for our feelings. Yet sometimes, suffering denies us even this most basic level of knowledge about why it afflicts us.

My friend Matthew has confided in me many times about his frustration in not being able to find the cause of his mental illness. Matthew, a doctoral student at one of the leading universities in the country, battles obsessive-compulsive disorder and depression in the midst of his research and teaching responsibilities. His obsessive-compulsive tendencies cause him to get easily distracted by scrupulously focusing on minute details of his work and behavior, while his depression sometimes keeps him chained to his small apartment in a state of despair. While psychotherapy and medication help Matthew cope with his mental illness, the specific causes remain hidden to him. They could have genetic, psychological, or neurological origins, but doctors can't tell him for sure. So Matthew struggles with the inability to name the silences that afflict him. He still asks, "Why?"

In addition to asking about the cause of suffering individually, we could pose the same type of question about the abundance of suffering that we experience collectively as a people. Why do we see men, women, and children stricken by poverty and dying in mass numbers with grossly inadequate access to food, water, and medical resources? It's sobering to realize that of the 6 billion people who inhabit our planet, almost half (2.8 billion) live on less than $2 a day while a fifth (1.2 billion) live on less than $1 a day.

Even in more affluent countries like the United States, nearly five percent of children are malnourished — a sad statistic in and of itself. But as much as half of the children in Latin America, South Asia, and Sub-Saharan Africa suffer from starvation. In cases like these, asking why leads us to a plethora of human causes — excessive consumption of resources by the rich, lack of education, failing economic structures, and oppressive governments — many of which could be improved to help alleviate the suffering to which they contribute.

Yet no matter how hard we work to alleviate suffering, it will always be present in the world to some degree. As the pope has taught us, suffering is the human condition, tightly woven into the fabric of our existence. Nevertheless, the pervasiveness and brutality of pain definitely makes us wonder why suffering has to be present among us at all. Why did suffering enter into the world in the first place? Why must it be an essential part of every human life?

As has been mentioned already, for an answer to that, all we need to do is crack open our Bibles to the third chapter in the Book of Genesis. According to the biblical account, suffering originated with the Fall — the sin of our first parents, who gave in to Satan's temptations. The problem of suffering exists indirectly through Satan, and directly through human sin.

Reflecting on this biblical explanation, Catholic writer G.K. Chesterton writes that if we put the evil that causes suffering under the microscope, we can see it for what it really is — a kind of poison, concocted by a human recipe of sin, as old as the human race itself. He elaborates:

> Men who wish to get down to the fundamentals perceive that there is a fundamental problem of evil. . . . The man in the mere routine of modern life is content to say that a modern gallows is a relatively humane instrument or that a modern cat-o'-nine tails is milder than an ancient Roman flagellum. But the original thinker will ask why any scourge or gibbet was ever needed, or ever even alleged to be needed? And that brings the original thinker back to original sin.[47]

When we ponder why suffering exists, we'll likely be led back to original sin, as Chesterton wrote. But it seems that when we try to interpret our suffering on a deeper, more personal level, the Fall proves to be an unsatisfying explanation for our pain. It strikes us as impersonal and detached from the intimate experiences of anguish that have often left us bludgeoned by the lashes of affliction.

Walk through the doors of a pediatric cancer ward, or attend the funeral of a teenager killed by a drunk driver. Talk to the veterans who have been wounded in combat and are haunted by memories of bloodshed. Recall the victims of the September 11 bombing of the World Trade Center and the millions of people who have been slaughtered as a result of genocidal madness. The biblical story of our first parents' sin and its harmful effects brings little consolation or meaning for such victims.

So, while the Fall is the Christian way of understanding how suffering came to be in the world, suffering is an intimately personal encounter with evil that seems to demand a personal explanation. We want to know the purpose of our pain and its significance for us, our loved ones, and our brothers and sisters throughout the world who hurt.

According to John Paul, this quest for personal meaning prompts us to ask from depths of our hearts, "Why? Why me? Why now? Why my wife, my father, my sister, my friend?"[48] Such questions voice our confusion about the purpose of our pain and the reasons we have to endure it. They grow out of our belief that life is not senseless but meaningful — a conviction which relentlessly drives us to seek the assurance that suffering has some purpose for us and isn't just wasted existence.

Seeking Purpose

Purpose is what gives direction and sensibility to the many decisions and actions that form our lives. It motivates and justifies virtually every activity we do. We eat and drink to nourish our bodies. We watch our favorite TV show to relax. We go to work every day to serve our community and earn money to provide for our needs. We give gifts to show our love and appreciation of others. We go to church to worship and draw closer to God. In most of what we do, we act with an intention to attain a goal and to fulfill specific purposes.

Sometimes, suffering follows this pattern when we endure trials sacrificially in order to achieve a greater good. We can think of sleep-deprived parents who patiently get up during the night to care for a new baby; men and women in the military who suffer injuries on the battlefield as they fight for their country; fatigued church leaders who persevere in their ministry in an understaffed parish; or those who endure the challenges of caring for the aging, sick, and dying.

In such cases and countless others, charity takes precedence over pain. Suffering is at least in part a voluntary act, because there is a deliberate decision to engage in activities with full knowledge that some form of discomfort will result. And to this extent, suffering can be meaningful as a means to an end — a self-offering of love that embraces pain in order to do good.

Yet much of the suffering we encounter brings us into circumstances we cannot control but that seem absurd — the chronic pain that plagues our every move, the depression and anxiety that weigh our hearts down, the inner turmoil that darkens our spirit, the unexpected loss of a loved one to death, the illness for which there is no cure. We find ourselves in situations like these that don't appear to serve any purpose other than to inflict pain and misery. Undoubtedly, we all have our stories that testify to how pointless suffering can be.

Recently a dear friend shared with me such a story about Annie, a vibrant young woman, a loving wife, and the mother of three children. About ten years ago, Annie and her little ones were driving home from the grocery store when she noticed a car stopped by the side of the road with the hood popped and smoke steaming out. There was no doubt that the driver was having car trouble.

So Annie decided to stop and help. She pulled over to the side of the road and got out of her minivan to ask the driver if she needed assistance. But as Annie was walking to the broken-down car, tragedy struck. A large truck plowed into the rear of Annie's van and catapulted it forward into her. Annie's three children inside the van, thankfully, survived the accident without major injury. But they witnessed the horror of their mother being crushed to death with the very vehicle that kept them safe.

What purpose could Annie's agonizing pain and death have possibly served? What sense does it make that Annie's husband would be left with the grief of being a widower at such a young age, or that her children would grow up without their mother? Why must Annie's kids forever endure the gruesome image of their mom being killed etched indelibly in their memories? It just doesn't add up.

John Paul writes that "in the eyes of the world, suffering, illness, and death are frightening, futile, and destructive."[49] Confronted by Annie's story, as well as our many other encounters with senseless suffering, "we find ourselves before an enigma, which we cannot honestly resolve by human means alone. It can make us cruel, it can embitter not only the one who is directly affected but also those who are close to him, and who, powerless to bring aid, suffer on account of that powerlessness."[50]

Here, the pope affirms that as we try to penetrate the mystery of suffering, we find that it ultimately defies rational explanation. Consequently, our experiences of pain over which we have no control can make us hardened and cynical, as our conception of the world changes from a place of order and purpose to one of chaos and confusion.

When Sarah and I were caught up in a whirlwind of grief after losing Sam and Bobby, many of our deep-seated beliefs — that had been rock-solid before their deaths — suddenly became like a thin sheet of ice, ready to crack and break apart under the weight of despair. We started to ask many "why" questions. Why would God allow our babies to die if He really loves us? Why should we keep believing and hoping in the midst of so much hurt? Why should we go on praying when so often our requests are met with silence? We felt so lost and began to question even our core convictions.

Suffering turns our world of meaning upside down. Anthropologist Clifford Geertz aptly describes this situation, stating that suffering presents us with an experience "... in whose face the meaningfulness of a particular pattern of life threatens to dissolve into a chaos of thingless names and nameless things."[51]

In *The Blood of the Lamb*, author Peter Devries tells the story of Don Wanderhop, who wrestles with the meaning of life as he witnesses the slow and agonizing death of his eleven-year-old daughter, Carol, to leukemia. While Devries wrote the book in the form of a novel, it describes his own experience of losing his little girl, Emily, to the same disease.

In one scene, Don has just checked Carol back into Children's Pavilion, the child-care unit of the hospital, because she has been experiencing headaches and eye trouble. A subsequent spinal tap shows that Carol's leukemia has moved into her spine, into which heavy doses of drugs will have to be injected. It is more bad news.

As Don waits for Carol in Children's Pavilion, he takes in what for him was a familiar scene: "the mothers with their nearly dead, the false face of mercy, the Slaughter of the Innocents."[52] It is there that he voices his crisis of meaning:

> We live this life by a kind of conspiracy of grace: the common assumption, or pretense, that human existence is "good" or "matters" or has "meaning," a glaze of charm or humor by which we conceal from one another and perhaps even ourselves the suspicion that it does not, and our conviction in times of trouble that it is overpriced — something to be endured rather than enjoyed. Nowhere does this function more than in precisely such a slice of hell as

a Children's Pavilion, where the basic truths would seem to mock any state of mind other than rage and despair.[53]

Surrounded by the scandal of dying children, including his own, Don Wanderhop has been beaten down by sorrow and frustration to the point that life looks meaningless. He has seen too much suffering not to despair — a feeling that reaches its climax with Carol's death, which results from an outbreak of an infection in the children's ward. Ironically, she dies just a short time after doctors have determined that her leukemia was in remission.

Mourning the loss of his little girl and unable to understand why, Don vigorously laments the senselessness of it all:

> How I hate this world. I would like to tear it apart with my own two hands if I could. I would like to dismantle the universe star by star, like a tree full of rotten fruit . . . Man is a mistake, to be corrected by his abolition, which he gives promise of seeing to himself. Oh, let him pass, and leave the earth to the flowers that carpet the earth wherever he explodes his triumphs. Man is inconsolable, thanks to that eternal "Why?" when there is no Why, that question mark twisted like a fishhook in the human heart.[54]

Wanderhop's raw, uncensored protest voices his inconsolable anxiety and discouragement with a world of suffering that, for him, appeared devoid of meaning. According to John Paul, such a dark emotional state often results when our quest for answers fails. The pope writes:

> The person who is afflicted . . . often wonders *Why must I endure this pain?* And almost immediately asks another question: *Why, what is the meaning of this suffering?* Not

finding an answer, he is despondent, because suffering becomes stronger than he is.[55]

This rock-bottom state of confusion and absurdity is when suffering is most lethal. Such is the view of holocaust survivor Dr. Victor Frankl. In *Man's Search for Meaning,* Frankl tells of his fight to grasp some kind of meaning amid the inhumane torture and killing that he, his family, and other prisoners endured in the Nazi concentration camps of World War II. Having been beaten, starved, and subjected to the other horrors of the camps, he reached the conclusion that human persons are ultimately not destroyed by suffering; they are destroyed by suffering without meaning.

Asking in Faith

John Paul informs us that the meaning of suffering, in its deepest sense, is an unsolvable mystery that transcends the power of our human reason. The question "Why do we suffer?" is an ultimate question that requires an Ultimate Teacher to lead us on the path of truth. In the words of the pope:

> Man does not put this question to the world, even though it is from the world that suffering often comes to him, but he puts it to God as the Creator and Lord of the world.[56]

Here, John Paul teaches us that turning to God in our quest for meaning in suffering is an act of faith. It affirms that God, who holds dominion over the world as its Creator and who fashioned each one of us in the womb, is the central source of meaning for our lives. To seek answers from God in the midst of our pain should not be mistaken as calling God's will into question or presuming that our finite minds can understand God's infinite wisdom. Rather, the pope assures us that asking

God "Why?" is a spiritual practice that we can feel comfortable doing because it actualizes our belief in who God really is.

Posing the question presupposes our faith in God as the Supreme Being who both rules the created world and also loves us and cares about our well-being. In faith, we assent to the truth that God is the Lord who is truly omnipotent (all-powerful), omniscient (all-knowing), and perfectly good. We believe that God knows of our suffering and the reason for it, possesses the power to help us overcome it, and wants what is best for us. Consequently, the pope informs us that it is right for us to raise our eyes to heaven and to call on God to help us make sense of our pain. He writes:

> Man can put this question to God with all the emotion of his heart and with his mind full of dismay and anxiety; and God expects the question and listens to it.[57]

John Paul assures us that we're heading in the right direction when we turn to God in our suffering. God expects us to ask "Why?" and recognizes that we rarely pose such a question in an emotional state of tranquility and composure, within the peaceful confines of sanctuary walls. No, God understands our humanity and expects that we'll come to Him as we truly are — beaten up on the street, sobbing and depressed, sleeves rolled up and temper flared — in desperate need of help on the one hand and ready to put Him on the spot for an answer on the other.

According to the pope, it is okay to lament our suffering. It is okay to tell God the feelings of our heart in honesty. In fact, it's more than just "okay" — this is what God wants from us: a real, personal relationship, free from conventions of etiquette that mask our true emotions with false smiles and pious prayers. True to the lamentation tradition of Israel, the pope assures us that God listens to us voice our pain as He listened to the Psalmist's prayer:

> How long, O LORD? Will you forget me for ever?
> How long will you hide your face from me?
> How long must I bear pain in my soul,
>   and have sorrow in my heart all the day?
> How long shall my enemy be exalted over me?
>
> Consider and answer me, O LORD my God;
>   lighten my eyes, lest I sleep the sleep of death;
> lest my enemy say, "I have prevailed over him";
>   lest my foes rejoice because I am shaken.
>
> — Ps. 13:1-4

Listening to the Psalmist's words, we hear both his faith in God's ability to help him and his frustration with the fact that he still hurts. God can help him but hasn't done so.

Such a situation — when our present condition of suffering seems irreconcilable with the God of our faith — poses great spiritual difficulties as we seek meaning from God and listen for His response. Indeed, if God is all-powerful, all-knowing, and perfectly good, why does He allow the excessive quantities of severe suffering to happen to us and to others throughout the world? Why would such a God not come to the aid of His creatures and intervene on their behalf when they are in serious pain?

In Fyodor Dostoyevsky's classic, *The Brothers Karamazov,* Ivan Karamazov pursues this line of questioning with his brother, Alyosha, a Russian Orthodox priest, in terms of why God would allow the abuse of children. In nauseatingly graphic detail, Ivan recounts stories of children who have been savagely tortured and murdered.

He speaks of an eight-year-old serf boy, who after throwing a stone that accidentally hurt the paw of a landowner's favorite dog, was given a death sentence. The landowner ordered that the boy be stripped naked in the cold and made to run, and then sent a pack of hounds after the boy to tear him to pieces. Another gruesome account describes how invading Turks in Bulgaria found pleasure in cutting unborn children from their mothers' wombs and killing children by shooting them at point-blank range. Still, a third example tells the repulsive story of a five-year-old girl whose parents physically abused her and left her to freeze to death in their outhouse.

Ivan can't make sense of why God wouldn't have come to the aid of these poor little victims. Reflecting on the story of the young girl, Ivan asks Alyosha:

> "Can you understand why a little creature, who can't even understand what's done to her, should beat her little aching heart with her tiny fist in the dark and the cold, and weep her meek unresentful tears to dear, kind God to protect her? . . . Do you understand why this infamy must be permitted?"[58]

Ivan's question is one we all share. Why doesn't God help the children? Why doesn't God help the rest of us? Certainly, God has the power to help us, is aware of our pain, and in His goodness, wants what is good for us. Simple logic draws us to these conclusions based on who God has revealed himself to be over the ages.

In the Judeo-Christian tradition, we have witnessed instances where God has wielded His wisdom, might, and love to alleviate the suffering of His people time and time again. For instance, in the Old Testament, the Exodus story tells of God's response to the desperate cry of His people, who were enslaved, abused, and exploited in Egypt. Revealing himself to Moses in the burning bush, God says, "I have seen the affliction of my people who are in Egypt, and have heard their cry . . . I know their suffering, and I have come down to deliver them out of the hand of the Egyptians, and to bring them up out of the land to a good and broad land . . ." (Ex. 3:7-8). Aware of His people's pain and feeling compassion for them, God came to Israel's rescue like a great warrior wielding plagues, death, and fire to destroy Pharaoh and his army.

Having walked on dry ground as the crashing waves behind swallowed the Egyptians, Moses and the Israelites found their faith in God vindicated. God liberated Israel from their oppression and proved that He was not only attuned to His people's needs but benevolent enough to want to help and powerful enough to do it. Reflecting on how God saved them from their misery, the Israelites could proclaim:

> I will sing to the LORD, for he has triumphed gloriously;
> > the horse and his rider he has thrown into the sea . . .
> The LORD is a man of war;
> the LORD is his name . . .
> Your right hand, O LORD, glorious in power,
> Your right hand, O LORD, shatters the enemy . . .
> You have led in your merciful love the people
> > whom you have redeemed,
> you have guided them by your strength to
> > your holy abode.
> > > — Ex. 15:1, 3, 6, 13

The New Testament testifies that the divine characteristics honored in Israel's song of praise have been personified in Jesus Christ, who as the Son of God made flesh, spent His career ministering to those who suffer. Of the numerous Gospel narratives that depict Jesus bringing healing to the afflicted, one of the most remarkable testimonies of His divine power, aware-ness of human pain, and compassion comes to us from the eleventh chapter of the Gospel of John.

The scene takes place in Bethany, near Jerusalem. Mary, who had anointed Jesus and washed His feet with her hair, and her sister, Martha, are distraught. Their brother, Lazarus, has fallen fatally ill, and it looks like he is going to die. So Mary and Martha summon Jesus, who loves Lazarus and his two sisters. Reading the narrative, we get the sense that Jesus is like an extended member of their family.

But during Jesus' journey to Bethany, Lazarus dies. And by the time Jesus arrives, Lazarus has already been laid to rest in a tomb for four days. Local members of the community are consol-ing Mary and Martha as they grieve over the loss of their brother. Upon seeing Jesus, the two sisters lament that Jesus couldn't have gotten there sooner to heal Lazarus: "Lord, if you had been here, my brother would not have died" (Jn. 11:21, 32), they say to him. But Jesus is too late to help. Lazarus is already dead.

Witnessing their sadness, Jesus is "deeply moved in spirit and troubled" (Jn. 11:33), to the point where on their way to the tomb, Jesus weeps. Once they arrive at the place where Lazarus has been buried, He calls for the removal of the stone covering the tomb, offers a prayer to His Father in heaven, and shouts, "Lazarus, come out" (11:43).

The Gospel tells us that the unthinkable happened next: "The dead man came out, his hands and feet bound with band-ages, and his face wrapped with a cloth" (Jn. 11:44). By the awe-some power and love of God, with whom all things are possible, Jesus turns Mary and Martha's grief into joy by reaching into the depths of eternity for Lazarus' soul and reuniting it again to his body. Jesus has brought Lazarus back from the dead.

We can only marvel at such an account that testifies to the kindness and might God exercised through His Son, Jesus. But it also begs the question, why doesn't Jesus help us in our present pain? Why won't He come to our rescue when we ask in prayer, as Mary and Martha asked so long ago? After all, Jesus promised that "whatever you ask in my name, I will do" (Jn. 14:13). Yet it seems these words are true only some of the time. Many of us who have prayed in faith for healing continue to suffer. In many cases, we have not been healed, and we wonder if God is really listening.

The Mystery of God's Response

In 1856, a baby boy named Justin Bouhort was born in France. From the beginning of his life, Justin had been frequently ill. By age two, he had never walked and was dying from tuberculosis, a disease consuming Europe. No cure existed for Justin, and it seemed he was another hopeless case.

Desperate to help ease the suffering of her little boy, Justin's mother took him to the grotto at Lourdes late one afternoon to implore the help of the Blessed Virgin Mary. With little Justin breathing shallowly in her arms, she approached the rock and whispered a prayer. She bathed Justin's emaciated body in the water, and then returned home.

Over the course of a few days, something miraculous happened. Justin began to walk, and weeks later, made a full recovery. After reviewing Justin's case, medical experts were amazed and found themselves lacking any scientific explanation. Biologically, the impossible had happened. Justin had his health completely restored and went on to enjoy a long, healthy life of seventy-nine years. It seems God answered a mother's prayer for her suffering son.

Such prayer success stories always cause a certain spiritual schizophrenia in me — thanksgiving for God's goodness in coming to the aid of someone in need, and confusion about why God helps the suffering only some of the time. Why does God say "yes" to some prayers to alleviate suffering and "no" to others?

If we look back over our story as Christians, God's benevolent response to prayers of petition is foundational. In the Gospels, Jesus frequently grants the requests of those in genuine need. Likening prayer to that of a child asking his or her parent for help, Jesus taught His disciples to confidently ask for the good things they need with the assurance that "whatever you ask in prayer, you will receive, if you have faith" (Mt. 21:22).

As the pain, frustrations, and trials of the human condition hurt us, we also offer our petitions to God in faith. Joy and thankfulness fill our hearts when God grants our prayer requests; desolation and sadness haunt us when our prayers evoke only God's silence. Either way, although we live in uncertainty about what God will do with our prayers for deliverance, we tend to expect the best.

No doubt reasons for this expectation include the past experience of having our prayers answered, or the Gospels' assurance that we will receive what we ask for, or the myriad miraculous accounts embedded in the Christian tradition. So, even as we recognize that some of our suffering is the result of human freedom wrongly exercised in sin, we still expect God's protection. If our prayers go unanswered, we ask, "Why didn't God rescue us from our suffering like He did for the Israelites and Mary, Martha, and Lazarus? Is our faith not great enough? Would a different type of prayer have been more effective?"

Such questions challenge our faith as we strive to reconcile who we believe God to be with our experience of suffering on earth. And our inability to find satisfying answers to them can take us down a lonely road of confusion, where God seems like a stranger. John Paul writes, "When pain obscures the mind and weakens the body and soul, God may seem very far away, and life can become an intolerable burden."[59]

Famed Christian author C.S. Lewis found himself at this place after his wife, Joy Gresham, died of cancer. In *A Grief Observed,* Lewis reflects on his pain as a widower. After describing the disabling effects of grief, which for him made engaging in even trivial daily activities like shaving and reading letters burdensome, Lewis turns his attention to spiritual matters:

> Meanwhile, where is God? This is one of the most disquieting symptoms. When you are happy, so happy that you have no sense of needing Him, so happy that you are tempted to feel His claims upon you as an interruption, if you remember yourself and turn to Him with gratitude and praise, you will be — or so it feels — welcomed with open arms. But go to Him when your need is desperate, when all other help is in vain, and what do you find? A door slammed in your face, and a sound of bolting and double bolting on the inside. After that, silence. You may as well turn away. The longer you wait, the more emphatic the silence will become. There are no lights in the windows. It might be an empty house. Was it ever inhabited? It seemed so once. And that seeming was as strong as this. What can this mean? Why is He so present a commander in our time of prosperity and so very absent a help in time of trouble?
>
> Not that I am (I think) in much danger of ceasing to believe in God. The real danger is of coming to believe such dreadful things about Him. The conclusion I dread is not "So there's no God after all," but "So this is what God's really like. Deceive yourself no longer".[60]

For Lewis, God became obscure in the dark night of grief. The fact that he turned to God for help and found none led him to reexamine his beliefs about who God really is. God didn't cure Joy's illness; God wasn't consoling Lewis in his grief. Instead, God just seemed to vanish from the scene — behavior which seemed uncharacteristic of the God Lewis believed in.

Like Lewis, we often feel abandoned by God in our pain. Suffering has a way of blinding our eyes to God's image and deafening our ears to His voice. Yet John Paul encourages us not to lose hope, for even if our suffering seems insurmountable and meaningless, we must believe that our quest for God and the meaning of our pain is worthwhile. It is not in vain. While we might not find easy answers along the way, we will find God — or God will find us. That is God's promise.

According to the pope:

> There are no easy answers for the questions posed by the minds and hearts of the afflicted. But we cannot find a satisfactory response without the light of faith."[61]

John Paul advises that in our search for meaning in suffering, "We must call on God, our Father and Creator, as the author of the Book of Wisdom did:"[62]

> With you is wisdom, who knows your works . . .
> Send her forth from the holy heavens . . .
> that she may be with me and toil . . .
> For she knows and understands all things.
>
> — Wis. 9:9, 11

LESSON 3

Not All Suffering Is Punishment

Molly and David Thompson and their four children belonged to the same parish as my wife and her parents in the 1990s. A young and vibrant family, the Thompsons enjoyed participating in parish activities and didn't know a stranger at Sunday Mass. Molly and David served on parish council and headed up the social justice committee, and their little ones could often be seen trotting up and down the church aisles during liturgies. All in all, the Thompsons were a devoted Catholic family whose faith shone forth in the way they loved each other and served their community.

But devastating news came for them in 1996. Nicholas, their second youngest child, developed a cancerous tumor behind his right eye when he was just a year old. Doctors advised Molly and David that the only way to prevent the cancer from spreading to the rest of Nicholas' tiny body was to surgically remove the tumor, and with it, his eye. Terrified at the thought of losing their precious little boy, Molly and David consented to the operation. The cure would come at a high price — blindness in one of Nicholas' eyes. But it was the only way to protect their son from death.

Nicholas went on to have a successful surgery and recovery. But in the midst of it all, the Thompsons would come to know even greater pain. David had been experiencing severe headaches for months and mentioned this to one of Nicholas' doctors. At the doctor's recommendation, David underwent a CAT-scan of his brain to make sure that there wasn't anything serious to worry about. However, the test results brought more bad news. A cancerous tumor was lodged in David's brain; like Nicholas, he would also require surgery to remove the mass. It was a life or death decision, and David chose to fight for his life.

A long surgery proved successful at extracting most of David's tumor, but a portion of it remained untouchable. Determined to stay alive for the family he loved, David spent the next year enduring the agony of chemotherapy while seeking alternative treatments from specialists around the world. He left no stone unturned in his quest to wipe out the residue of cancer in his brain. But in the end, his efforts didn't save his life, and David finally lost his battle with cancer at the age of thirty-six. Death forced him to leave the wife, children, and community he loved and who loved him.

In the wake of Nicholas' surgery, which left him with a glass eye, and the tragedy of David's untimely death, Molly desperately began asking why she and her family deserved so much suffering. What had they done wrong? Why was God punishing them? Did her sins or David's sins warrant such a harsh sentence from God? And even if they did, why should the kids, who were innocent, be punished?

Molly believed that she and her family had lived in a way that was pleasing to God. They prayed, followed God's commandments, loved each other, and served their community as best they could. So she just couldn't understand where the justice was in what had happened to her family. Their agony didn't seem fair. Distraught at the possibility that they were being punished unjustly by God, she wrestled with the problem of innocent suffering.

Getting to Know Job

John Paul points us to the Book of Job as the "most vivid expression" of our struggle to understand suffering when it feels like an undeserved punishment from God.[63] The book begins by introducing Job, a man who is "blameless and upright, one who feared God, and turned away from evil" (Job 1:1). Job is a family man with ten kids — seven sons and three daughters — and has prospered so much that he is considered "the greatest of all the people of the east" (1:4). But Job doesn't let his worldly success inflate his ego with pride. He remains humble before God, and wakes up early each morning to offer sacrifice to God to atone for any sins that his children might have committed.

Job's faithfulness doesn't escape God's notice. In the next scene, angels appear before God in the heavenly court. Ironically, among them is Satan, who informs God that he has just come back from roaming the earth. God, knowing Satan will have seen this for himself, asks:

> "Have you considered my servant Job, that there is none like
> him on the earth, a blameless and upright man, who fears
> God and turns away from evil?"   (1:8)

Satan has noticed, all right. But, while conceding that Job's conduct on earth has pleased God, Satan is critical of Job's motives. He suggests that Job's blessings are the reason for his faithfulness to God:

> "Have you not put a hedge about him and his house and
> all that he has, on every side? You have blessed the work
> of his hands, and his possessions have increased in the
> land."   (1:10)

So Satan proposes a wager: he bets that if Job is stripped of his good fortune, he will curse God (1:11). Surprisingly, God accepts Satan's challenge and places all that Job has in Satan's power to destroy at will — the only exception being that Satan may not afflict Job himself.

This results in disaster for Job back on earth. A series of messengers visit Job and bring him tragic news — his servants have been murdered, his livestock have perished in a blazing fire, and his children have been crushed to death by a great wind that knocked over the house in which they were staying.

Stripped of his offspring and means of wealth, Job doesn't sin or blame God for his pain. In humility, he tears his robe, shaves his head, and falls to his knees to worship God with these words:

> "Naked I came from my mother's womb, and naked I shall return; the LORD gave, and the LORD has taken away; blessed be the name of the LORD." (1:20)

Because Job worships God in the midst of trial and grief, he proves that his righteousness is pure and doesn't hinge on the earthly comforts that God has given him.

When Satan returns to the heavenly court, God confronts Satan with the truth about Job:

> "He still holds fast to his integrity, although you moved me against him, to destroy him without cause." (2:3)

God affirms that Job has proven his faithfulness and is innocent of any behavior that would justify the suffering by which he was tested. But Satan remains unconvinced about Job's character.

Believing that Job will certainly turn his back on God if made to suffer greater afflictions, Satan proposes another bet to God:

> "All that a man has he will give for his life. But put forth your hand now, and touch his bond and his flesh, and he will curse you to your face."   (2:4-5)

While Job's faith withstood the loss of his children and possessions, Satan wants to attack Job's own flesh with pain. Again God accepts Satan's challenge and gives him the power to wound Job, but with the exception that Job must not to be killed.

So Satan descends to earth and smites Job with "loathsome sores from the sole of his foot to the crown of his head" (2:7). Having lost all of his children, money, and now his health, Job has gone from riches to rags. He uses a piece of pottery to scrape his wounds as he sits poor, sickly, and alone on a garbage heap. In Job's time, society ostracized those who were seriously ill — not only for fear that they would spread disease, but because they carried the stigma of being great sinners punished by God. So Job must assume his miserable new role as a social outcast whose illness has ended his normal way of life and now threatens to do the same to his body.

At this point, Job's wife gets fed up. She grieves the loss of their children and possessions, and now she has to watch her husband live out his days diseased and anguished. She and Job have been robbed of the life they once loved and shared together. With her faith in God shaken, she says to Job in despair:

> "Do you still hold fast your integrity? Curse God, and die."
>   (2:9)

As if Job's suffering isn't bad enough, he loses the support of his wife — the one person left he could count on. Yet even though she has turned against God, Job holds his ground:

> "You speak as one of the foolish women would speak. Shall we receive good at the hand of God, and shall we not receive evil?"   (2:10)

In humility, Job accepts whatever God sends into his life, whether good or bad.

Having heard of the calamities that have befallen Job, his friends, Eliphaz, Bildad, and Zophar, come to visit and comfort him. However:

> ... when they saw him from afar, they did not recognize him; and they raised their voice and wept; and they tore their robes and sprinkled dust upon their heads toward heaven.   (2:12)

Moved with pity, they decide to stay with Job for seven days, and no one speaks a word during that time. Job's suffering is too horrible to even talk about.

However, after seven days of agony, Job's patience finally gets pushed to the limit. He can't contain his frustration any longer and breaks the silence by cursing his birth:

> "Let the day perish wherein I was born ... Let that day be darkness! May God above not seek it, nor light shine upon it. Let gloom and deep darkness claim it. Let clouds dwell upon it; let the blackness of the day terrify it."
>
>   (3:3-5)

Suffering has destroyed the meaning of Job's existence, and leads him to conclude that a life consumed by pain is not worth beginning in the first place:

> "Why did I not die at birth, come forth from the womb and expire? Why did the knees receive me? Or why the breasts, that I should suck? For then I should have lain down and been quiet; I should have slept; then I should have been at rest . . ."   (3:11-13)

> "For my sighing comes as my bread, and my groanings are poured out like water . . . I am not at ease, nor am I quiet; I have no rest; but trouble comes."   (3:24-26)

Filled with anguish, Job despises his life in which his only hope is death — the only way to end his misery. Such an existence, he believes, is a cruel joke that should never have been played on him or humanity:

> "Why is light given to him who is in misery, and life to the bitter in soul, who long for death, but it comes not, and dig for it more than for hidden treasures; who rejoice exceedingly, and are glad, when they find the grave? Why is light given to a man whose way is hidden, whom God has hedged in?"   (3:20-23)

No sooner does Job finish lamenting, however, than his buddies suggest that they know the reason for his pain. Job suffers, in their opinion, because he is guilty of serious sin for which God is punishing him. Confident that Job is in a state of denial, the men decide to initiate an intervention on his behalf. So they take turns charging Job with wrongdoing and urging him to admit his guilt. Eliphaz says to Job:

"Think now, who that was innocent ever perished? Or where were the upright cut off? As I have seen, those who plow iniquity and sow trouble reap the same. By the breath of God they perish, and by the blast of his anger they are consumed."   (4:7-9)

Bildad follows:

"Does God pervert justice? Or does the Almighty pervert the right? . . . If you will seek God and make supplication to the Almighty, if you are pure and upright, surely then he will rouse himself for you and reward you with a rightful habitation."   (8:3, 5-6)

Job's friends, rejecting his innocence, instead try to convince him that God will take away his suffering if only he will repent of his sin.

Suffering Sent by God?

Reflecting on these charges, John Paul comments that Job's three old friends assume he "must have done something seriously wrong."[64] They see Job's misery through the prism of the law of retribution in which God, the Just Judge, rewards the righteous with peace and prosperity on earth but punishes the wicked with suffering. Job's friends, according to the pope, believe that all suffering is "punishment for a crime; it is sent by the absolutely just God and finds its reason in the order of justice."[65] The only God that Eliphaz, Bildad, and Zophar know is the God who "repays good with good and evil with evil."[66]

Sometimes, we think of the relationship between God and our suffering in a similar way. When trial and tribulation befall us, we have a tendency to scour our consciences in an effort to judge whether or not our guilt justifies our pain. We try to determine if we have given God a reason to punish us.

But what a challenge it is to really know for sure. How thoroughly must we analyze our moral history during the evaluation process? Should we interpret our current suffering as punishment for a sin we committed years ago, or just yesterday? Are we being disciplined now for all of our sins, a select group of sins, or just one particular sin? And what about sins that God has forgiven — are they still subject to punishment?

Such questions smack of ambiguity, but are we crazy for asking them? Is there any solid evidence in divine revelation that supports the correlation we make between our suffering, our moral flaws, and God's justice?

Rewind to the time of Job. Deeply ingrained in the consciousness of anyone who lived in that era was the notion that suffering on earth was a divine punishment for sin. This belief was an integral part of Israel's tradition, dating all the way back to the creation account in the Book of Genesis, and threads through the pages of the entire Old Testament. Genesis tells how Adam and Eve's rebellion against God's law in the garden was the offense that incurred severe penalties — namely, the sentence on them and all living creatures that made the world subject to suffering and death. From then on, the precedent for the law of retribution was set: disobey God and suffer the consequences.

Moses has this principle in mind in the Book of Deuteronomy, when he exhorts the Israelites to obey God's commandments in the Promised Land, so as not to incur the punishments of disobedience:

> "See, I have set before you this day life and good, death and evil. If you obey the commandments of the LORD your God . . . by loving the LORD your God, by walking in his

ways, and by keeping his commandments and his statutes and his ordinances, then you shall live and multiply, and the LORD your God will bless you in the land which you are entering to take possession of it. But if your heart turns away, and you will not hear, but are drawn away to worship other gods and serve them, I declare to you this day, that you shall perish; you shall not live long in the land which you are going over the Jordan to enter and possess. I call heaven and earth to witness against you this day, that I have set before you life and death, blessing and curse . . ."

— DT. 30:15-19

Moses makes it clear that fidelity to God's law is a life-or-death decision. God rewards those who are obedient to His commandments with blessings and prosperity but punishes the disobedient with suffering and death. In this sense, God justly enforces the law of retribution and gives to each person what she or he has merited — either good or evil.

Divine justice, writes John Paul, is "one of the fundamental truths of religious faith."[67] At the same time, the practice of rewarding good behavior and punishing wrongdoing appeals to our basic moral sensibilities. In the pope's words, it "manifests a conviction also found in the moral conscience of humanity: the objective moral order demands punishment for transgression, sin, and crime."[68]

Reflecting on Israel's experiences of suffering in the Old Testament, we also see that God's punishments go beyond balancing the scales of justice. They have an educational and rehabilitative purpose. John Paul explains that "punishment has a meaning not only because it serves to repay the objective evil of the transgression with another evil, but first and foremost because it creates the possibility of rebuilding goodness in the subject who suffers."[69]

Here, the pope describes how suffering can serve as a kind of divine discipline that helps correct human faults — a belief also well represented in the Old Testament. The sacred writer of the Book of Proverbs, for instance, offers this counsel:

> My son, do not despise the LORD's discipline or be weary of his reproof, for the LORD reproves him whom he loves, as a father the son in whom he delights.
>
> — PROV. 3:11-12

In this passage, God is likened to a good father whose punishments, which often result in suffering, are given to his children out of love.

John Paul also reminds us that one of the central purposes of God's discipline is to bring sinners to repent and accept God's mercy.[70] Such is the interpretation given much later in the second Book of Maccabees. During the reign of the Seleucid kings in the second century B.C., the Jews in Jerusalem were brutally oppressed. In an effort to wipe out Judaism and replace it with Greek culture and religion, the Seleucids slaughtered the Jews, plundered the Temple, and erected a statue of Zeus on the Temple altar. Remembering these horrors, the sacred writer of 2 Maccabees writes:

> Now I urge those who read this book not to be depressed by such calamities, but to recognize that these punishments were designed not to destroy but to discipline our people . . . he [the LORD] never withdraws his mercy from us. Though he disciplines us with calamities, he does not forsake his own people.
>
> — 2 MAC. 6:12, 16

Such biblical testimonies are grounded in the belief that God does, in fact, inflict suffering on His people to punish them when they are guilty of sin — not only to restore justice, but as the pope teaches us, "to strengthen goodness both in man himself and in his relationships with others and especially with God."[71] This way of thinking about God and suffering forms the lens through which Job views his own situation:

> "For the arrows of the Almighty are in me;
>> my spirit drinks their poison;
>> the terrors of God are arrayed against me . . .
> I was at ease, and he broke me asunder;
>> he seized me by the neck and dashed me to pieces;
>> he set me up as his target, his archers surround me.
> He slashes open my kidneys, and does not spare;
>> he pours out my gall on the ground." (6:4, 16:12-13)

While Job can accept that his suffering is from God, however, what sends his mind into a dizzying tailspin of confusion is that he doesn't believe he is guilty of any sin that would warrant such harsh retribution. Nagging him at every moment is the same question that Molly Thompson asked in the midst of her suffering: "What have I done to deserve this?" Desperate to find an answer, Job beseeches God:

> "Teach me, and I will be silent;
>> make me understand how I have erred." (6:24)

Job knows he isn't perfect, but to the best of his knowledge he is innocent of any transgressions that would justify punishment as severe as his suffering. In Job's eyes, the scales of justice look tipped in favor of his punishment, which greatly outweighs his offenses:

"O that my vexation were weighed, and all my calamity
laid in the balances! For then it would be heavier than the
sand of the sea . . ."   (6:2-3)

Job believes that no sin he has ever committed could justify discipline as terrible as his present suffering.

Most of us have probably been in a similar place — suspi-
cious that God is punishing us with suffering but convinced
that our pain exceeds our guilt. The result can be confusion
and spiritual unrest when we must choose between convicting
ourselves unjustly or entertaining the blasphemous notion of a
God who isn't fair. So we're left wondering whether our suffering is punishment or not.

Surely there are times when innocence amid suffering is
easy to see. Take the suffering of children, for instance. Before
the age of reason, children aren't even capable of making any
moral decisions for which they could be declared guilty.
Although all of us, including our children, have inherited the
guilt of original sin, a child who is unable to distinguish right
and wrong can't be guilty of personal sin. So if personal guilt is
a prerequisite of divine punishment, and a child can't be guilty
of personal sin, then it only makes sense to conclude that God
doesn't punish children with suffering. Our children can only
be victims of suffering that they don't deserve.

But what about the rest of us, who *can* be held accountable
for our personal sins? How do we reach an innocent verdict
about ourselves? Certainly, none of us stand wholly innocent of
moral flaws. But neither are we 100% sinners — guilty to the
core. Surely, a mixture of innocence and guilt makes up our
moral character.

Nevertheless, it seems the more serious our suffering, the
easier it is for us to feel that our afflictions are unjust. The
agony of battling a life-threatening disease, the torment of

severe pain, the grief of mourning a tragic death, the misery of starvation and poverty — these and other grave forms of suffering decry innocence on behalf of the ones who must endure them. When we experience extreme suffering, we conclude with relative certainty, along with Job, that we're innocent. For only the most unspeakable acts of sin could warrant such intense forms of anguish to counterbalance the scales of justice.

Such talk is utter nonsense to Job's friends, who believe suffering and guilt go hand in hand. For them, things are simple. Serious suffering results from serious sin; repentance is the only way to be cured — end of story.

In the biblical narrative, Eliphaz, Bildad, and Zophar think Job suffers because he hides his sin under a huge boulder of pride. After all, if God is truly just, and suffering is God's punishment for sin, then Job must be guilty of sin. Armed with the strength of this religious conviction, Job's friends again challenge his innocent plea and ask:

> "How long will you say these things, and the words of your mouth be a great wind? Does God pervert justice? Or does the Almighty pervert the right?"   (8:2-3)

God's justice makes Job's claim of innocence untenable to his friends, who see hidden in Job's plea the blasphemous implication that it is God who is guilty for persecuting Job without just cause.

Zophar goes so far as to completely minimize Job's pain by asserting that if justice were truly served, his afflictions would be even greater than they are:

> "For you say, 'My doctrine is pure, and I am clean in God's eyes.' But oh, that God would speak, and open his lips to

you, and that he would tell you the secrets of wisdom! . . .
Know then that God exacts of you less than your guilt
deserves."   (11:4-6)

Job tries to share his pain and voice his confusion to his
friends, but his words fall on deaf ears. They have already
reached a verdict — Job suffers because he has sinned.

Wading Through the Depths of Mystery

In his quest to understand his suffering in light of his faith in
God, Job finds himself living in a mystery he can't resolve. He
believes God justly punishes sinners with suffering. But Job
also believes himself to be innocent. Consequently, frustration
overtakes Job as he fails to put these two beliefs together suc-
cessfully. He stands in misery, shell-shocked by what has happened to him. Suddenly the God whom he has always trusted
to be on his side and to protect him stands holding the bloody
sword that pierces him. With his faith shaken and heart broken,
Job says:

> "God will not turn back his anger . . . If I summoned him
> and he answered me, I would not believe that he was listen-
> ing to my voice. For he crushes me with a tempest, and
> multiplies my wounds without cause."   (9:13, 16-17)

Job doubts that God cares about his pain or hears his
prayers anymore. At the same time, Job can't deny his experience of innocent suffering, which for him proves that God uses
His power to punish the guiltless as well as the guilty. As a
result, Job concludes that this state of affairs renders God's justice null and void:

"Though I am innocent, my own mouth would condemn me; though I am blameless, he would prove me perverse. I am blameless; I regard not myself; I loathe my life. It is all one; therefore I say, he destroys both the blameless and the wicked."   (9:20-22)

So, disillusioned by sorrow, angst, and disappointment, Job begins to walk down into an even darker valley as he imposes evil and sadistic qualities onto God. He says:

"When disaster brings sudden death, he mocks at the calamity of the innocent. The earth is given into the hand of the wicked . . ."   (9:23-24)

Job questions God's goodness and starts to think that God even delights in persecuting the innocent.

According to John Paul, Job's spiritual anguish results from his myopic view of the relationship between suffering and God. Job, like his friends, understands every instance of earthly suffering to be an exercise of God's justice. Sin is the event that brings about an effect — punishment from God.

But the problem with universalizing this religious definition of suffering always comes when Job judges himself to be innocent, and at the same time, judged guilty by God. John Paul writes that by his very existence as a righteous man who also suffers, Job "challenges the truth of the principle that identifies suffering with punishment for sin. And he does this on the basis of his own opinion. For he is aware that he has not deserved such punishment, and in fact speaks of the good he has done in his life."[72]

Believing that the severity of his suffering far exceeds his guilt, Job can't reconcile his experience with the just God he believes in — a God who begins to look like a divine monster who punishes innocent victims like him without cause. Job says in protest:

> "Behold, I cry out, 'Violence!' but I am not answered; I call aloud but there is no justice . . . He breaks me down on every side, and I am gone, and my hope has he pulled up like a tree."   (19:7, 10)

In our personal relationships, most of us can recall situations where we have felt victimized and wounded when someone we trusted to love us and look out for our best interests let us down. Once the damage has been done, we can't help but question the character of the one who betrayed our trust. Consequently, our relationship with that person usually weakens and without reconciliation just falls apart entirely.

When it comes to dealing with suffering, we often relate to God in a similar way. God speaks to us in Revelation as a personal God who desires an intimate, loving relationship with us. Listening to God's Word, we trust God when He says that He loves us as children, and we believe God looks out for us as any good parent would for his or her little ones. In response to God's call to friendship, we try to nurture our relationship with God through prayer, worship, and service, and we strive to honor God by doing things that please Him.

But when we suffer and believe we are innocent, we tend to feel like God has let us down. We wonder why we hurt if God loves us and has the power to protect us. A relationship defined by love is one where persons are committed to do what is best for the other, so it seems impossible that God would want what is best for us and still punish us with suffering when we don't deserve it. Even less likely does it seem that God would allow us to endure pain that He could have ultimately prevented. We ask God, "Lord, how could you do this to me?" Such an honest prayer expresses the heartache and anger that comes with feeling mistreated by a loved one.

When our experiences don't reconcile with what we believe to be true about God, we, like Job, experience a kind of cognitive dissonance. We're left to ask how God can be who He claims to be — a good, loving, and just parent who cares for us as children — when so many of the Nicholases, Davids, Mollys, and Jobs of the world continue to suffer.

It is at this point of our reflection that equating suffering with punishment becomes especially toxic for our life of faith. If we believe that our suffering is evidence that God treats us unfairly, we start to go down the same spiritual path Job did. We feel betrayed by God. We rebel against the hypocrisy of God's justice and challenge God's love for us. We put God on trial for crimes against humanity and begin to think that God is the adversary who afflicts us wrongly. In the end, all we can do is join our voices to Job's indictment and call on God to account for his wrongful actions:

> "Oh, that I had one to hear me! (Here is my signature! Let the Almighty answer me!) Oh, that I had the indictment written by my adversary! . . . I would bind it on me as a crown; I would give him an account of my steps; like a prince I would approach him."   (31:35-37)

So how does God answer such a prayer? In Job's case, God responds by speaking in the wind. While Job has called upon God to take the witness stand and justify his conduct, God will do no such thing. Instead, God answers with a barrage of questions that challenge Job's pretentious attitude and limited view of reality. God replies:

"Who is this that darkens my counsel by words without knowledge? . . . Where were you when I laid the foundation of the earth? Tell me, if you have understanding. Who determined the measurements — surely you know!" (38:2, 4-5)

God identifies himself as the universe's Creator whose wisdom far surpasses that of Job, a mere creature. God goes on to point out the magnificent intricacies of the natural world that He designed — the light of dawn and the darkness night; the heavens filled with clouds and stars that tower over the earth; the intermingling of elements to form precipitation and wind; the animal kingdom sustained by the fruits of the earth. Having reminded Job of his transcendence and power, God calls on Job to respond:

"Shall a faultfinder contend with the Almighty?
He who argues with God, let him answer it."   (40:2)

Job is at a loss for words. He doesn't know the details of how the universe came to be or what kind of plan charts its course through history. Clearly, only God possesses this knowledge. So Job must admit his ignorance in humility:

"Behold, I am of small account; what shall I answer you? I lay my hand on my mouth. I have spoken once, and I will not answer; twice, but I will proceed no further." (40:4-5)

Job goes from being an accuser of God to a passive listener. Yet despite his humble disposition, Job doesn't admit any guilt worthy of being punished with suffering. And while God never accuses Job of sin, God also doesn't give Job a straight answer about whether he deserves to suffer.

At the same time, God challenges the charge that He is guilty of mistreating Job unjustly. God asks Job:

> "Will you even put me in the wrong?
> Will you condemn me that you may be justified?"   (40:8)

In response to Job's accusations, God asserts his divinity:

> "Have you an arm like God,
>   and can you thunder with a voice like his?
> Deck yourself with majesty and dignity;
>   clothe yourself with glory and splendor.
> Pour forth the overflowings of your anger,
>   and look on every one that is proud, and abase him.
> Look on every one this is proud, and bring him low;
>   and tread down the wicked where they stand.
> Hide them all in the dust together;
>   bind their faces in the world below.
> Then will I also acknowledge to you,
>   that your own right hand can give you victory."
>   (40:9-14)

Again, God turns the tables on Job and calls his human logic into question. Job doesn't understand how God created and governed the natural world, nor does he fully grasp the relationship between God and suffering. Based on the teachings of his religious tradition, Job has come to view all human suffering as an exercise in God's justice. But God reveals that Job must expand his theology because God's ways don't always fit neatly into the box of human rationality. In the words of John Paul, Job must look upon his suffering with new eyes and realize that it "must be accepted as a mystery," which he is "unable to penetrate completely by his own intelligence."[73] The challenge for Job is to bow down before the mystery of God's transcendence in faith when answers don't come easy.

Having heard God's answer to his lamentations, Job seems to find a path to a spiritual place of humble acceptance. He resigns himself to God's will and confesses his limited knowledge as a child of God:

> "I know that you can do all things, and that no purpose of yours can be thwarted . . . I have uttered what I did not understand, things too wonderful to me, which I did not know." (42:2-3)

While Job still doesn't understand why he suffers, he comes to know peace by surrendering himself to God, whose plan for him is much bigger than he can see. Trusting in God and overwhelmed by his presence, Job prostrates himself and seeks reconciliation:

> "I had heard of you by the hearing of the ear, but now my eye sees you; therefore I despise myself, and repent in dust and ashes." (42:5-6)

Job's prayer of repentance doesn't withdraw his initial plea of innocence but expresses his renewed faith and his sorrow for doubting God. Holding tight to the belief in his innocence, Job has been right all along. He didn't do anything deserving of his suffering — a fact confirmed when God vindicates him before his friends. God declares that Job has spoken rightly of Him while Job's friends, who purported to be messengers of religious truth, have incurred God's wrath (42:7).

In the end, it is Job's prayer that compels God to show mercy to his friends. And, as a final act of vindication, God restores Job to health, reunites him with his family, and returns his wealth and possessions in even greater quantities.

Putting the Pieces Together

So what can we take way from the Book of Job to help us? What difference does Job's story make in our lives as sufferers?

John Paul responds that Job teaches us an essential lesson about the relationship between God, humanity, and suffering — namely, that not all suffering is punishment for sin. The fact that Job suffered intensely, even though he was righteous, sets a biblical precedent for the reality of innocent suffering in the world. We learn from Job that not every earthly affliction we face is an agent of God's justice. The pope informs us:

> While it is true that suffering has a meaning as punishment, when it is connected with fault, it is not true that all suffering is a consequence of a fault and has the nature of punishment.[74]

Where the law of retribution would see all suffering as a kind of divine whip that scourges us for our sins, the pope warns that this point of view has its limitations. He writes:

> The Book of Job does not violate the transcendent moral order, based upon justice, as they are set forth by the whole of Revelation . . . At the same time, however, this book shows with all firmness that the principles of this order cannot be applied in an exclusive and superficial way.[75]

In Job's story, God overturns any religious tradition that sees every occurrence of suffering as a divine punishment for human sin.

John Paul encourages us to find comfort in the truth that we often suffer innocently before God. Suffering doesn't equal guilt. We don't have to ask, "What did I do wrong?" at the first sign of pain. According to the pope, we have God's word on this:

> Revelation, which is the word of God himself, with complete frankness presents the problem of the suffering of an innocent man: suffering without guilt.[76]

We know from Job's story that he didn't deserve the terrible suffering that tormented him. In the words of John Paul, suffering in Job's case "has the nature of a test."[77] The problem for Job is that unlike the readers of his story, who know God is testing him, he is incapable of seeing the cause of his anguish. Even though Job is convinced of his innocence, he must endure his suffering within a mystery he can't solve.

All of us live in that same mystery, as we try to allow our faith to illuminate the meaning of suffering for us. We want to know what God has to do with our pain. Is God the perpetrator, inflicting it on us? Is God just allowing it to happen? Are we, too, being tested by God? These are difficult questions — honest questions. But thinking through them, even within the context of the story of Job, doesn't give us any crystal-clear answers. Instead, we learn from the divine voice in the wind that God's ways aren't our ways and often extend beyond the reach of human reason. Within the mystery of divine providence, which governs and sustains the world, things don't always make sense. The innocent suffer. The guilty thrive. And we don't understand why.

Living amidst this paradox, we learn from Job that God's justice can't be pigeonholed into conceptions of human justice. Tallying up our sins to see if they reconcile with the sum of our sufferings will lead us down the wrong road to draw false conclusions about ourselves and God — a lesson Jesus himself taught His disciples (see Lk. 13:1-5; Jn. 9:13). This kind of spiritual cost accounting didn't ultimately give Job any answers, nor will it do so for us. Thus, the pope writes:

> [While interpreting suffering as punishment] has a fundamental and transcendent reason and validity, at the same time it is seen to be not only unsatisfactory in cases similar to the suffering of the just man Job, but it even seems to trivialize and impoverish the concept of justice which we encounter in Revelation.[78]

In our quest for the meaning of suffering, John Paul calls us to look deeper into the riches of God's Word beyond the Book of Job. While Job's story takes us deeper into the human experience of innocent suffering and establishes its precedent in our religious tradition, the story also leaves some issues unresolved.

Reading the narrative through a Christian lens, we probably are struck by God's willingness to send suffering upon Job in response to Satan's challenge. This seems out of character for God — afflicting human beings with suffering as part of a supernatural wager doesn't seem like something the God of Christian faith would do. It might leave us wondering if God is testing us with suffering in a similar way.

At the end of the story, we also read that because of Job's faithfulness and repentance, God removes Job's suffering and restores all that he has lost on earth. Such beneficent actions on God's part testify to His goodness and inspire us to hope in His loving desire to heal us. At the same time, God's willingness to reverse Job's suffering could also lead us to question why God has not done the same for us, even though we have prayed for help, repented of our sins, and remained faithful to God as Job did.

Finally, and most importantly, Job's story doesn't reveal any explicit answers about the meaning of suffering. While Job finds his faith strengthened by God's vindication of him and the assurance that divine providence is working for a good he doesn't understand, by the end of the story, Job still hasn't grasped any detailed spiritual insight into his own experience of suffering.

And so, John Paul encourages us to read the Book of Job for the good news that not all suffering is punishment. Like Job, we can suffer innocently. Having learned this lesson, the pope invites us to continue our study of suffering because Job's story "does not yet give the solution to the problem."[79] Revelation has much more to teach us, in the person of Jesus Christ.

LESSON 4

God Wills Salvation, Not Suffering

Everything happens for a reason. We have all probably heard or voiced this proverb at some point in our lives. It reassures us that our experiences, no matter how joyful or horrible, have a bigger meaning — even though we might not understand what exactly that meaning is.

As Christians, we might say that everything happens according to God's purposes. Our faith in divine providence — God's benevolent guidance of all things for the good — compels us to view God as a Divine Artist who uses our experiences to sculpt us into holy masterpieces called saints. But how does our suffering fit into this process? Is it part of God's plan for us? Like Job, we all seek a reason for our suffering and often try to find a place for it in God's will.

In January of 2004, after Sarah and I buried Bobby, we shut ourselves off from the world. Overwhelmed with sorrow and anger, we didn't want to talk to anyone and withdrew from social activities. Going to church on Sundays was a struggle; even squeezing prayer out of our desolate souls felt like birth pangs, as it seemed that God had abandoned us. Wounded by our grief, we just wanted our son back again. But there was nothing we could do but try to manage our pain.

During this time of loss, we were blessed with the kindness of family and friends who tried to console us. Our parents took us out to dinner, did our dishes, walked our dog, and just sat still with us as we struggled to keep breathing in and out. It was a wonderful gift, feeling so loved.

I also remember how some of our distant friends and relatives, not knowing quite what to say, tried to comfort us with encouraging spiritual talk: "Well, you know that God has His reasons" . . . "Everything happens according to God's plan" . . . "God just couldn't wait to be with Bobby." These sayings, while coming from well-meaning people who desperately wanted to help us, just poured gas on the flames of our pain and confusion.

But was there any truth in these sentiments? I began to critically reflect on my own assumptions about them. I thought about the pain Bobby must have felt in my wife's womb as his umbilical chord strangled him to death. I thought about our grief, weighing on our hearts like a giant millstone. Was all of this agony really God's will — just some big test for us like the one sent to Job? Or worse, could God be punishing us?

As I prayed about this question, I recalled other concentrated experiences of suffering — the slow, harrowing death of my dad to colon cancer; the millions of innocent people killed in natural disasters, genocide, and terrorist attacks; the scores of religious martyrs; the poor, the sick, and the dying. Certainly it is possible that God could have sent portions of this suffering in order to serve some greater divine purpose. But how could a God who initiated or allowed such catastrophes really be on the same side as the victims?

Embracing God's Love

According to John Paul, we find insights into this deep question of faith only in Jesus' revelation of God's love, "the ultimate source of the meaning of everything that exists."[80] Jesus came into the world to show us the magnificent love of God, who doesn't desire our pain but our salvation — our eternal liberation from the evil of suffering. "This answer," says the pope, "has been given by God to man in the Cross of Jesus Christ."[81] Last February, when I was watching the Super Bowl, the camera panned over to a fan holding a sign. Painted on it in big black letters was *John 3:16*. The biblical passage referenced reads, "For God so loved the world that he gave his only-begotten Son, that whoever believes in him should not perish but have eternal life." There, in the midst of a sea of frenzied football fans, stood a lone prophet proclaiming the central dogma of Christianity — the love God has for us is so big, so radical, that He became one of us and died on the Cross to bring us into the joy of His life forever.

Jesus shared this good news with Nicodemus and His followers two millennia ago. Since then, the message has become so ingrained in our Christian rituals and literature that we sometimes gloss over it without embracing its true significance. John Paul calls us to look at Jesus' words recorded in John 3:16 afresh, with new eyes, and remember this most essential truth for our lives — Jesus' death on the Cross was God's supreme act of love for us. The Cross is the ring that weds us to the ever-living God who created us out of nothing; it is the font that pours forth God's grace to cleanse us of our sins and renew our spirit; it is the key that opens the heavenly gates to an everlasting future where our tired, aging bodies will be raised in glory and happiness. Amazed by such an awesome gift of love, each of us can marvel with St. Paul that Jesus "loved me and gave himself for me" (Gal. 2:20).

The pope encourages us to keep this Gospel truth ablaze in our hearts as we suffer. Suffering is an evil that hurts us. But our salvation, accomplished by Jesus' passion and death, expresses God's loving desire to free us from suffering for all eternity. According to the pope, this is what salvation means. To save, he says, is "to free man from evil, which bears within itself the definitive and absolute perspective on suffering."[82]

In other words, God gave his Son to free us from worst form of suffering we could ever imagine — the loss of eternal life.[83]

Even more terrible than the most agonizing physical pain and horrific death on earth is being forever separated from God. John Paul explains:

> The opposite of salvation is not, therefore, only temporal suffering, any kind of suffering, but the definitive suffering: the loss of eternal life, being rejected by God, damnation.[84]

Through Jesus' passion and death, God saved us from hell and opened His arms to the world with an invitation to share in His life and love.

This vast mystery of the Cross, hidden in divine providence, evokes the image of the grain of wheat in the Gospel of John. There Jesus says, "Unless a grain of wheat falls into the earth and dies, it remains alone; but if it dies, it bears much fruit" (Jn 12:24). In His own parabolic way, Jesus uses this metaphorical saying to assure His disciples that His death will not be in vain. Like the grain that dies, Jesus knows He will bear the fruit of salvation by dying on the Cross for our sins.

According to Christian tradition, something much bigger than the bloody death of an innocent man was happening behind the scenes at Calvary. Jesus' death was God's sword, wielded in the cosmic struggle between good and evil, to fatally pierce through the armor of sin and death that separated the human race from God. In the pope's words:

> In his salvific mission, the Son must therefore strike evil right at its transcendental roots from which it develops in history. These transcendental roots of evil are grounded in sin and death . . . at the basis of the loss of eternal life. The mission of the only-begotten Son consists in conquering sin and death.[85]

Scholars have written volumes explaining how the Cross, as the ultimate sign of God's love, prevailed in this cosmic struggle. Catholic theologian Hans Urs von Balthasar states that through the Cross, God's "eternal plan is executed to clean away the whole terrible mess of the world's sin and consume it in the fire of suffering love."[86] Karl Rahner, S.J, another prominent Catholic theologian of the last century, describes the Cross as:

> ... the *signum efficax*, the efficacious sign, of the redeeming love that communicates God himself, because the cross establishes God's love in the world in a definitive and historically irreversible way.[87]

Such reflections, while inspiring and thought-provoking, can feel somewhat detached from my practical understanding. I find myself asking, "Why did it have to go that way? Why did Jesus have to get nailed to a cross to set things right? Couldn't God have given us eternal life in some other way?" The fact that Jesus had to die in order to redeem the world seems so unfair and tragic, even though the end result of salvation is certainly to my benefit. But throughout the New Testament writings is the teaching that Jesus' sacrificial death on the Cross was necessary for salvation — a notion that finds its roots in Old Testament prophecy.

Nearly 3,000 years ago, God called the prophet Isaiah to deliver a message of hope to the people of Israel, who had been taken captive by the Assyrians. This captivity, Israel thought, was their just punishment from on high — the rod of God's judgment because of their unfaithfulness to the covenant. But Isaiah writes that despite Israel's disobedience, God desires reconciliation.

The prophet foretells of the Servant of the Lord, an innocent "man of sorrows," who will bear Israel's transgressions through suffering. In so doing, the Servant will make atonement to God for Israel's sins and restore the relationship between God and His chosen people. In the words of Isaiah:

> He had no form or comeliness that we should look at him,
>   and no beauty that we should desire him.
> He was despised and rejected by men;
>   a man of sorrows, and acquainted with grief;
> and as one from whom men hide their faces
>   he was despised, and we esteemed him not.
> Surely he has borne our griefs
>   and carried our sorrows;
> yet we esteemed him stricken,
>   struck down by God, and afflicted.
> But he was wounded for our transgressions,
>   he was bruised for our iniquities;
> upon him was the chastisement that made us whole,
>   and with his stripes we are healed.
> All we like sheep have gone astray,
>   we have turned every one to his own way;
> and the LORD has laid on him the iniquity of us all.
>
> — Is. 53:2-6

Christianity identifies Jesus as the personification and fulfillment of this "man of sorrows" foretold by Isaiah. According to John Paul, meditating on Isaiah's prophecy:

> . . . [can lead us to] identify the stages of Christ's Passion in their various details: the arrest, the humiliation, the blows, the spitting, the contempt for the prisoner, the unjust sentence, and then the scourging, the crowning with thorns and the mocking, the carrying of the Cross, the crucifixion and the agony. [88]

This man of sorrows wounded for our iniquities is none other than Jesus himself.[89]

John the Baptist made this confession of faith as he baptized sinners and preached repentance in Bethany. Upon seeing Jesus, John proclaimed, "Behold, the Lamb of God who takes away the sin of the world!" (Jn 1:29). John recognized Jesus as Israel's long-awaited Messiah, God's anointed one, who would bring reconciliation between God and the world.

But reconciling God and His people came at the highest cost — the blood of the Lamb. St. Paul writes that Jesus "emptied himself, taking the form of a servant . . . And being found in human form he humbled himself and became obedient unto death, even death on a cross" (Phil. 2:7-8). God the Father sent the Son in human form to pay the price for our sins with the sum of His own life. This total self-gift was the powerful way that God showed His love for us. Indeed, "By this we know love, that he laid down his life for us" (1 Jn. 3:16).

Sometimes, it's easy to lose sight of the magnitude of God's love poured out for us on the Cross, which all too often becomes an abstract symbol of religious identity rather than the splintery wooden frame to which Jesus, bearing our sins, was nailed. A reality check came for me when I first watched the 2003 film *The Passion of the Christ.*

Depicting the last hours of Jesus' life, which culminated in His passion and death, the movie delivers in high-definition surround sound a shockingly realistic depiction of the violence that He suffered. See the film and it's like you're back on the streets of first-century Jerusalem, witnessing the extreme psychological and physical torment that Jesus underwent. Mel Gibson, the director, said he wanted this experience to jolt viewers into developing a deeper appreciation of the Paschal event.

The film certainly achieved that goal for me. The movie's lifelike portrayal of Jesus' crucifixion has helped correct my tendency to over-theologize the Cross in such a way that focuses primarily on its spiritual meaning, divorced from the agony Jesus experienced. A more personal and real-life understanding of the brutal way that Jesus bore the world's sin has helped me venerate the Cross for its saving effects without obscuring their cause — God's sacrificial love, poured out in Jesus' blood.

Jim Caviezel, the actor who played the role of Jesus, recalled in interviews how he shared the experience of the Cross even while making the film. During the shooting of the crucifixion scene in Italy, perched high on a giant wooden cross, he suffered hypothermia in the cold wind, and extended hours of hanging brought on episodes of suffocation. At one point, a thunderstorm blew in, and one of the crew noticed that Caviezel had smoke coming from his ears. He had been struck by lightning!

As he went through these personal sufferings on the movie cross, Caviezel remembered the indignation that swelled inside of him as people on the set stood down below drinking coffee, laughing, and going about their business — not paying much attention to his welfare. In that experience of agony and abandonment, Caviezel found solidarity with Jesus.

Jesus' crucifixion paints a dark portrait of how the world met God's love with mockery and contempt expressed in whips, thorns, and spikes. It also proved that God's love couldn't be reduced to any kind of "eye for an eye" attitude that would have warranted retaliation for the injustice and hatred that led to the Cross. No, Jesus responded to His suffering with love for the Father, whom He obeyed; love for the world, which He saved; and love even for His executioners, whom He forgave.

As we journey into the mystery of suffering, John Paul calls us to remember this love as proof that God is on our side. Scripture teaches us:

> In this the love of God was made manifest among us, that
> God sent his only-begotten Son into the world, so that we
> might live through him. In this is love, not that we loved
> God but that he loved us and sent his Son to be the expia-
> tion for our sins.
>
> — 1 Jn. 4:9-11

God sent Jesus to save the world from suffering. In this,
the pope writes:

> Love is manifested, the infinite love both of that only-
> begotten Son and of the Father who for this reason gives his
> Son. This is love for man, love for the "world": it is salvific
> love.[90]

The Complexity of the Cross

The Cross is a knotty reality to unravel, especially when examined in light of the problem of suffering. We believe that Jesus
fulfilled a divine mission to save us from the powers of sin and
death through His sacrificial passion and death. At the same
time, believing that Jesus gave His life as ransom presupposes
that there was a debt to be paid on our behalf. But to whom? If
the creditor is God, does this mean that God required the ter-
ribly gruesome death of Jesus on the Cross? And if so, what
does this say about God and His will for our personal suffering?

In my own heart, I have observed a reluctance to accept
Jesus' suffering as God's will. Certainly, I find consolation in
believing that God spared no expense, even his own Son, to
save me. But I don't like thinking that God could have willed
such terrible suffering for Jesus. A God who demands blood
doesn't fit my idea of love, which is patient, kind, and works for
the good of the beloved. Did God really call for Jesus' passion
and death as the purchase price of our salvation?

Judging from the writings of some contemporary theologians, the popular answer on the street today is "no." Many will mince no words about their view that God didn't require Jesus' suffering because such an evil intention is incompatible with a God of love. They argue that if God is truly "Abba" ("Daddy" in Aramaic), then he must be a purely positive and loving Father who would never will anything negative like the pain and death that Jesus experienced. Such a perspective makes it easy to conclude that the Cross wasn't part of God's plan at all. Instead, it resulted from human sin playing out within the historical circumstances in which Jesus found himself.

We often hear this idea tossed around in the secular media and even in some Christian publications. Hardly a Lenten season goes by without magazine stories, introduced by images of Jesus hanging on the Cross, with headlines such as "Did Jesus Really Have to Die?" The articles will then go on to explain that Jesus was crucified because He challenged the religious and political institutions of his day. Put quite simply, Jesus was an inspiring yet controversial religious prophet who made enemies who conspired to kill Him — end of story. The new religious "insight" that we are asked to accept is that God didn't will the death of Jesus as a blood sacrifice to atone for our sins, as Scripture would have us believe; Jesus' martyrdom was the result of human hatred and mistakes. But it was in no way an intended event within God's saving plan.

Such attempts to free God of any responsibility for Jesus' suffering appeal to our innate sense of divine justice and love. How a good God could will something as horrible as crucifixion to befall Jesus is a difficult question to tackle.

Yet Scripture, which we profess to be God's Word, tells us that God did in fact require atonement for human sin, and that the Cross fulfilled that condition. Jesus is the sacrificial Lamb who takes away the world's sin, says John the Baptist (Jn. 1:29).

Like the paschal lamb that saved the Hebrews at the first Passover in Egypt, Jesus would also "give his life as a ransom for many" (Mt. 20:28). We see this same paschal motif again when Jesus shares the cup of wine with His disciples at their last Passover meal together. He says, "Drink of it, all of you; for this is my blood of the covenant, which is poured out for many for the forgiveness of sins" (Mt. 26:27-28). Centuries later, John would reflect on the meaning of Jesus' death on the Cross and describe it as "the expiation for our sins, and not for ours only but also for the sins of the whole world" (1 Jn. 2:2).

In light of such passages, it seems that contemporary doctrines which treat Jesus as merely a human person oppressed by God and his countrymen fail when subjected to a Scriptural litmus test. They simply don't agree with the testimonies about Jesus' death and our salvation in the Church's inspired writings.

As we read the Scriptural interpretations of Jesus' Cross, we see lurking in the background the mysterious truth that Jesus is a divine Person who is both God and man. Jesus is the Word, who existed from the beginning of time, and Creator of the universe. He is also the man of flesh and blood who wept at the death of His friend Lazarus, screamed at the merchants disgracing the Temple, and sweated profusely in terror of His impending trial and execution. This is the complexity of who Jesus is.

At the same time, John Paul writes that it is Jesus' unique identity as the *God-man* that empowers His death with saving value and differentiates Him from every other religious martyr in history.[91] The popular modern conception of Jesus as a great prophet who was persecuted because His message ruffled some feathers in the first-century Mediterranean world doesn't tell the whole story. Jesus is a *divine person* in human form. Therefore, all of His actions, including His death on the Cross, have taken on both a human and divine meaning. As Christians, we face this tension between Jesus' humanity and divinity along with the mystery wrapped up therein.

If we see Jesus as only a human person victimized in history because of His radical lifestyle and teachings, or merely as an innocent man oppressed by a God who required blood, we cross over the boundary from dynamic orthodoxy to heretical fiction. We fail to identify Jesus for who He really is: the Word of God incarnate who came to save the world in fulfillment of the Scriptures (cf. Jn. 1:14). According to John Paul, Jesus' death on the Cross is not evidence of the Father's wrath being taken out unjustly and horrifically on His innocent Son. Jesus is not God's victim; Jesus is the God-man who has become a victim on our behalf. The pope emphasizes that it is precisely because Jesus is both God and man that He can offer the atoning sacrifice that saved us from sin and death:

> He who by his Passion and death on the Cross brings about redemption is the only-begotten Son whom God "gave." And at the same time, this *Son who is consubstantial with the Father suffers as a man.* His suffering has human dimensions; it also has unique in the history of humanity — a depth and intensity which, while being human, can also be an incomparable depth and intensity of suffering, insofar as the man who suffers is in person the only-begotten Son himself: "God from God." Therefore, only he — the only-begotten Son — is capable of embracing the measure of evil contained in the sin of man: in every sin and in "total" sin, according to the dimensions of the historical existence of humanity on earth.[92]

If we search the history books, we find heroes who have suffered sacrificially and given their lives in love of God and others. But only Jesus could infuse a world of sin with God's saving love as the Word incarnate, who knew of the divine plan of salvation and the role of His Cross in accomplishing it. Scripture and the Church teach us that the Cross was no accident contingent only on historical circumstances; it was God's ordained instrument of salvation, which Jesus knew about and fully embraced with loving obedience to the Father. John Paul explains:

> Christ goes toward his own suffering, aware of its saving power; he goes forward in obedience to the Father, but primarily he is united to the Father in this love with which he has loved the world and man in the world.[93]

If we look at how Jesus' suffering and death play out in the Gospels, we see two supernatural plots converge — the plot of Satan and the plot of God. The Gospel of Luke credits the death of Jesus to the plot of Satan, who inflamed hate in the hearts of the chief priests and other religious leaders who conspired to have Jesus killed. But Jesus was in no way naïve about what was happening. On the contrary, during the Passover meal, Jesus knew that Judas was against Him and said to His disciples, "Truly, I say to you, one of you will betray me" (Mt. 26:21). Likewise, there were no question marks in Jesus' mind about His imminent suffering and crucifixion: "You know that after two days the Passover is coming, and the Son of man will be delivered up to be crucified" (Mt. 26:2). According to Scripture, Jesus foretold the events that would lead Him to the Cross:

> "Behold, we are going up to Jerusalem; and the Son of man will be delivered to the chief priests and the scribes, and they will condemn him to death and deliver him to the Gentiles; and they will mock him, and spit upon him, and scourge him, and kill him."
>
> — MK. 10:33-34

Such a bloodcurdling prediction from the lips of Jesus was a hard pill for His disciples to swallow. Upon first hearing this prophecy, Peter couldn't believe it. He took Jesus aside and expressed his disapproval. But Jesus replied, "Get behind me, Satan! For you are not on the side of God, but of men" (Mk. 8:33). From Jesus' vehement response, we see that Peter's good intentions threatened to undermine another plot juxtaposed with Satan's scheme to have Jesus killed — God's plan of salvation.

As the Scriptures strongly testify, getting in the way of God's plan is a mistake. Upon His arrest in the Garden of Gethsemane, Jesus reprimanded one of the disciples, who, in an attempt to protect Him, sliced the ear of the high priest's slave:

> "Do you think that I cannot appeal to my Father, and he will at once send me more than twelve legions of angels? But how then should the Scriptures be fulfilled, that it must be so?"
>
> — MT. 26:53-54

Jesus knew that His saving mission included the Cross, which He freely accepted, saying, "Shall I not drink the cup which the Father has given me?" (Jn. 18:11).

Time and time again, Scripture tells us that Jesus was confident in the saving power of His suffering. According to John Paul, Jesus knew:

> . . . precisely by means of this suffering he must bring it about "that man should not perish, but have eternal life." Precisely by means of his Cross he must strike at the roots of evil, planted in the history of man and in human souls. Precisely by means of his Cross he must accomplish the work of salvation.[94]

Here, the pope confirms for us that Jesus' decision to offer His life as ransom for a sinful world in humble obedience to the Father's will ignited the light of salvation. By way of the Cross, the dark abyss of suffering became a window of grace through which God's saving love could permeate souls and bring them to eternal life. So as we seek to discover the meaning of our own suffering, we find hope in our God who doesn't desire pain and death but who loves us and sent His Son, Jesus, to save us from them.

Saved But Still Suffering

A few years ago on a warm, hazy June afternoon, I was sporting my tux and meeting my beautiful bride, Sarah, at the altar to say "I do." God's presence, which seems to come and go through the ups and downs of my spiritual walk, felt so tangible that summer's day. It was as though God's hand was on my shoulder like a proud parent beaming with joy. I can say unequivocally that my wedding was among the most blessed experiences of my life, as I pledged my love to such a beautiful woman of God.

Looking back, I remember the romantic vision I had about what the first year of marriage would look like. I pictured candlelit dinners, long walks in the park, remodeling our fixer-upper house, and starting our family. These were the dreams that I longed to actualize as Sarah and I became a "we." And what better way to initiate this blissful beginning as husband and wife than a dream honeymoon?

After twelve hours of travel from our home in Cincinnati, Ohio, we finally arrived at our cozy love nest nestled high in the mountains of picturesque Victoria Island, Canada. Both of us craved the relaxing amenities of our hotel to help us shake off the stress of our day-long expedition and many months of wedding planning.

But then things took an unexpected turn. As I was checking in at the desk, I suddenly felt the room begin to spin. It was as if our hotel was a giant tilt-a-whirl whipping us around in a circle. Never had I been so dizzy.

Sarah took my arm to support me as I stumbled to our room. Having endured a rigorous day of travel, I attributed my symptoms to fatigue. I thought surely a little rest would soon get me back on my feet. One hour went by, then two hours, three, and four, but my dizziness kept getting worse. By midnight, I was flat on my back in bed. Even lifting my head from the pillow sent me into a state of complete nausea. Talk about bad timing! This was definitely not how I pictured the first night of our honeymoon.

The next day, my condition didn't improve. So Sarah chauffeured me down the twisty mountain road to the local doctor, who diagnosed me with vestibular neuronitis, a fancy term that means "your inner ear is messed up and you're going to be really dizzy for an undetermined period of time."

My dizziness ended up incapacitating me for our entire ten-day stay. All of our plans had to be canceled, as I lay imprisoned in our hotel room. Every tinge of romance had quickly been sucked out of our honeymoon. And poor Sarah was stuck taking care of me rather than hiking the beautiful country or enjoying the tourist attractions that surrounded us.

When our time in Victoria Island ended after what seemed like an eternity in honeymoon hell, I was still extremely dizzy. My doctor advised us that I was unfit to fly home because the altitude shifts in the plane could damage my inner ear, which was already weakened. So we rented a car. And Sarah, being the saint that she is, drove me all the way from Canada to our house in Ohio — 2,500 miles over three days and nights of driving nineteen hours at a time and catching only a few hours of sleep in budget motels. I felt disgustingly sick the whole way. Sarah was dead tired. The entire honeymoon experience was utterly miserable. But we finally made it home.

During our first year of marriage, my condition was slow to improve and dashed many of our hopes for what our honeymoon period would be like. Our new lifestyle looked so different than the one we had anticipated — confinement to the house, frequent doctor visits, MRI tests, physical therapy, anxiety about my prognosis, and worst of all, inability to sleep in the same bed (I had to sleep sitting up in a chair for three months). Through it all, Sarah was my rock who stood by me — loving, hoping, patiently waiting, and sacrificing. But dealing with my illness was physically and emotionally painful for both of us.

We all have our stories of suffering. Such experiences present us with the tough reality that while the Cross saves us from eternal suffering, it doesn't liberate us from the evil of earthly pain here and now. Suffering continues to be a universal problem we encounter every day on earth — the toil of work, the heartache of love, the anguish of illness, the turmoil of sin, and the sting of death. Suffering is just part of the ebb and flow of life.

But why doesn't God help us in our present pain? If God loves us and wills our salvation, why won't He come to our rescue and free us from suffering right here and now?

As Christians, we struggle with this mystery bound up in our experience of God, who sometimes heals our suffering but in other circumstances seems unwilling to help. So we have to face the reality of an unpredictable God who is involved in the world — doing good and allowing evil — in ways we often don't understand. I think there is no better evidence of this than the Cross. How unreasonable is it that our salvation, God's ultimate gift of love to us, could flow out of such a grave act of pain and injustice as Jesus' passion and death?

Perhaps we, like Job, can find some peace in the midst of this mystery by bowing down before God's transcendence and accepting that we'll never fully understand all there is to know about God and divine providence. Some things are beyond reason's grasp. As St. Paul says, our earthly life only allows for a dim, partial vision of things (cf. 1 Cor. 13:12). We don't get any simple answers about why God heals some of our hurts and not others. God has not revealed this to us. And just as children can't understand all of the reasons for their parents' decisions, it's difficult for us not knowing why God responds as He does to our suffering.

At the same time, coming to such a conclusion doesn't free us from the pain of living in a suffering world. Suffering haunts us from the moment our life begins and strikes its strongest blow in death, which John Paul describes as the "dissolution of the entire psychophysical personality of man."[95] Death tears us down in a complete way. In the pope's words, it literally dissolves us from the world. He writes that death is the "definitive summing-up of the destructive work in the bodily organism and in the psyche."[96] Anyone who is dying or has witnessed someone die knows just how true these words are.

Twenty years ago, when I was nine years old, I remember watching colon cancer slowly disintegrate my dad's bodily and mental functions in the months leading up to his death at the tender age of thirty-six. The last night I saw him alive, he was in his hospital room, propped up by pillows and connected to several beeping medical devices, but still alert and unbelievably hospitable for a man on his deathbed. I'll never forget how one of his major concerns while Mom and I were there visiting with him was whether or not we were thirsty. He kept asking, "How about something to drink?" "No thanks, Dad," I quickly replied. "No, no, Bob. I'm fine, thanks," Mom said with tears in her eyes. His love for us was still at work even in the throes of his fight to break free from the imminent bonds of death. But as Dad lay there half-conscious, just hours before his death, it was clear his body and spirit were fading away.

According to John Paul, this destructive work of death finds its roots in original sin, after which God declares, "you are dust and to dust you shall return" (Gen. 3:19). Death is not merely a biological reality or natural phenomenon. Faith tells us that death has a deep theological meaning. It is like a disease that our first parents contracted from the poison of sin and that subsequently spread to their descendants (cf. Rom. 5:12). In other words, death and suffering are consequences of human sin. But St. Paul reminds us that where sin led to condemnation and death for us, Jesus brings acquittal and life (cf. Rom. 5:18).

Jesus is God's cure for suffering and death. According to John Paul:

> [Jesus] blots out from human history the dominion of sin . . . beginning with Original Sin, and then he gives man the possibility of living in Sanctifying Grace . . . he also takes away the dominion of death, by his Resurrection beginning the process of the future resurrection.[97]

Where Adam's legacy is sin and death, Jesus' legacy is righteousness and life. Through God's love for us expressed in Jesus' saving Cross and glorious rising, we become heirs not of Adam's decadent legacy but of the resurrection and joy that the Son of God offers us.

While our present pain might be terrible, so much more than we think we can bear, John Paul assures us that Jesus gives us good reason to hope:

As a result of Christ's salvific work, man exists on earth *with the hope* of eternal life and holiness. And even though the victory over sin and death achieved by Christ in his Cross and Resurrection does not abolish temporal suffering from human life, nor free from suffering the whole historical dimension of human existence, it nevertheless *throws a new light* upon this dimension and upon every suffering: the light of salvation. This is the light of the Gospel, that is, of the Good News.[98]

The Good News of Jesus assures us that, although we live in a world of suffering, we can hope in God's promise that salvation has already begun and will one day lead to everlasting freedom from pain. It gives us confidence that God's love, not suffering, will have the last word for us. It shows us God's work in history to undo the powers of evil that hurt us. It consoles us with the truth that God is on our side.

God Is on Our Side

Seeing suffering through faith-colored glasses often proves difficult. Pain can devour our spiritual sensibilities in the flames of disappointment, sadness, anger, and despair. In our moments of suffering, seconds turn into hours, hours turn into months, and months turn into years of struggle to survive the creative whims of evil that challenge our hope in the promises of God.

If we look into the narratives of Jesus' life, we see that even He wasn't impervious to the cold, sharp strike of suffering's steely hand. As the Son of God who assumed a human nature, He was like us in every respect except sin. This means He took on the full burden of suffering that comes with being human, including the humiliation of being rejected by His own people on top of the horror of public execution. John Paul comments:

During his public activity, he [Jesus] experienced not only fatigue, homelessness, misunderstanding even on the part of those closest to him, but, more than anything, he became progressively more and more isolated and encircled by hostility and the preparations for putting him to death.[99]

The world of suffering granted Jesus no exemption. Yet ironically, suffering became the human experience through which God chose to express His love and to draw close to us in His Son. The pope writes:

God the Father has loved the only-begotten Son, that is, he loves him in a lasting way; and then in time, precisely through this all-surpassing love, he "gives" this Son, that he may strike at the very roots of human evil and thus draw close in a salvific way to the whole world of suffering in which man shares.[100]

According to John Paul, the truth that God loved us so much that he sent His Son to suffer with us, and by doing so to save us from our sins, "radically changes the picture of man's history and his earthly situation."[101] In Jesus, we not only see God's love for us poured out in flesh and blood, but we also discover suffering as the common ground on which we can stand with our Lord and Savior, who knows the painful dimension of being human firsthand.

The great ancient philosopher, Aristotle, taught that we are political and social beings. As such, we tend to be drawn to others who have shared similar experiences as us, especially during times of crisis. We find consolation from fellow sufferers who can relate to our pain because they have felt it, too. At the same time, the burden of our own suffering can feel lighter when we receive the comfort of solidarity and communion from our brothers and sisters, whose empathy and encouragement become a great source of strength.

God offers us His companionship in His Son, Jesus, who as Emmanuel (God with us) has walked in our shoes in suffering and in death. In this most intimate way, God chose to extend His loving arms to save us and pull us into His eternal embrace. Such is the nature of love — to bring unity between the lover and the beloved.

Jesus assures us that God's love is incompatible with disengagement. Even if we have no or little support from others when we hurt, we don't suffer alone, because our Lord is with us. Opening our eyes to the reality that Jesus' footprints are right beside us on the dark road of suffering, we can avail ourselves of His company. We can also find solace in remembering that God has touched what we're going through in the body of our Savior.

But sometimes, God's presence seems so distant. There are moments when we hurt so badly that we question if God is really with us. We wonder, "Where is God?" Certainly such a question about God's whereabouts could be heard from the lips of family members who lost loved ones in the September 11 World Trade Center disaster, from Auschwitz prisoners and the millions of other victims of genocide, from fathers and mothers forced to leave their family in death, from grief-stricken parents whose children have died, and from the seriously ill. Indeed, it is a question asked by all of us who have been badly wounded by suffering.

In his memoir, *Night,* holocaust survivor Elie Wiesel recalls searching for God as he witnessed the public hanging of a young boy in a Nazi concentration camp. As Wiesel and other prisoners walked by the boy during his execution, they saw how his young body was still quivering as the rope's stranglehold refused his struggle for air. In that moment, one prisoner asked in utter despair, "Where is God now?" Wiesel recounts how he heard a voice inside of himself responding: "Where is He? Here He is — He is hanging here on this gallows. . . ."[102]

One can only imagine Wiesel's feelings during such a horrific experience, but his words give insight into the Christian response to the question of God's presence amidst suffering. Where is God? The Christian must answer, "Here He is — He is hanging here on this cross." God makes His love and presence known to all who suffer through the vulnerability and pain of Jesus during His passion and death. Suffering is an experience God shares with us in Jesus. It is a point of communion. In this sense, Jesus' words, "I am with you always, to the close of the age" (Mt. 28:20), hold special meaning for us as sufferers.

One way we can remember that God accompanies us as we suffer is to meditate on the Cross. This is the spiritual practice that mystic Julian of Norwich practiced as she lay in excruciating pain on what she believed was her deathbed (although later, she would be miraculously healed). She found that keeping her eyes fixed on the crucifix and meditating on the Lord's passion gave her comfort and strength in her time of pain.

Such a gruesome sight — the thorns digging into Jesus' skull, the slash in His side, and blood-covered nails piercing His hands and feet — is a vivid picture of human weakness. Jesus is the victim of hatred, abuse, mockery, and torture as He hangs on the cross, gasps for air, and feels the pangs of death. Beholding the crucifix, we realize that Jesus knows what we know about suffering and so much more. It is here, at the foot of the Cross, that we can meet with Jesus and receive His friendship as a co-sufferer.

And yet at this same place beneath the Cross, we also behold God's strength and wisdom. Scripture often gives us divine truth tangled up in paradoxes: the last shall be first; lose your life and find it; the foolish are wise; the weak are strong;

the poor are rich; the humble will be exalted. True to fashion, St. Paul writes to the Corinthians that Christ crucified is truly the manifestation of God's wisdom and power:

> For the word of the cross is folly to those who are perishing, but to us who are being saved it is the power of God . . . For the foolishness of God is wiser than men, and the weakness of God is stronger than men.
>
> — 1 COR. 1:18, 25

Paul teaches us that in the weakness of the Cross, we find God's providential power that saved the world. According to John Paul:

> On the Cross, Christ fully accomplished his mission: by fulfilling the will of the Father, he at the same time fully realized himself. In weakness he manifested his *power,* and in humiliation he manifested all *his messianic greatness.*[103]

How naïve and foolish this doctrine appears to the naked eye, sundered from the lens of faith. Nevertheless, God demonstrated his might not in muscular images, like thunderbolts and lightning high atop a mountain, but in the suppleness of human flesh, the vulnerability of love, and the anguish of death. Such apparent weakness serves as the guardian of power in God's plan of salvation. Leave it to the mysterious wisdom of God to transform the cross — the Romans' favorite death device — into the universal instrument of salvation that opened wide the gates of heaven. For it was upon the Cross that Jesus stretched out in cruciform as God's supreme act of passionate love for us.

Alongside the Cross, we also see God's gigantic love for us and closeness to us in our suffering in the many scriptural accounts depicting Jesus' compassion for people who hurt.

John Paul writes that Jesus was "sensitive to every human suffering, whether of body or soul."[104] In Jesus, we see not only a fellow sufferer who embraced the many pains and struggles of the human condition with us, but also a great lover of sufferers, who dedicated much of His life to bringing healing and comfort to them.

The Gospels abound with stories about how Jesus helped the afflicted. He opened blind eyes, made lame legs walk, sanctified demonized souls, and even raised lifeless bodies from the dead. It seemed that wherever Jesus appeared, suffering vanished. The Gospels say that the people "brought him all the sick, those afflicted with various diseases and pains, demoniacs, epileptics, and paralytics, and he healed them" (Mt. 4:24). Word spread quickly that Jesus possessed power over suffering:

> And great crowds came to him, bringing with them the lame, the maimed, the blind, the dumb, and many others, and they put them at his feet, and he healed them.
>
> — Mt. 15:30

Such an abundance of these signs remembered in Scripture testify to Jesus' special love for suffers in those communities where He lived and traveled. Like the Good Samaritan, Jesus opened His eyes and heart to those in pain, and He responded with care.

Among the stories portraying Jesus' compassion for sufferers, one tells how Jesus brought a mother's only son back to life:

> Soon afterward he went to a city called Na'in, and his disciples and a great crowd went with him. As he drew near to the gate of the city, behold, a man who had died was being carried out, the only son of his mother, and she was a

widow; and a large crowd from the city was with her. And when the Lord saw her, he had compassion on her and said to her, "Do not weep." And he came and touched the bier, and the bearers stood still. And he said, "Young man, I say to you, arise." And the dead man sat up, and began to speak. And he gave him to his mother.

— Lk. 7:11-15

This narrative always comes alive for me because I'm my mom's only son and have experienced the amazing gift of her love for over thirty years. I'm also a parent who has said goodbye to two beloved children who died. I think this is why the relationship of love between parent and child, and the painful experience of loss in the story, feels so tangible and familiar to me.

Reflecting on the passage, I imagine the breathtaking elation the mother in the story must have felt when Jesus raised her son from death. Most of us will never have such an experience. Yet I find great comfort in Jesus' deep concern for the suffering of this mother and son, and the extraordinary compassion He showed to them.

Such accounts of Jesus' healing ministry characterize God's love for sufferers and also foreshadow a time to come, when suffering will perish. Scripture scholars tell us that Jesus' miracles herald the arrival of the kingdom of God on earth, that Jesus' work to overcome suffering in His public ministry inaugurates the reign of God in which holiness, happiness, and eternal life will dismantle sin, suffering, and death.

This was Jesus' message of hope proclaimed during His Sermon on the Mount to the poor, hungry, sad, rejected, hated, and ostracized — all called blessed in God's kingdom (cf. Mt. 5:3-12; Lk. 6:20-23). Jesus perceived the problem of human pain, and He promised vindication, peace, and joy to the suffering masses. Through words and deeds, Jesus made it clear that, while suffering continues to exist on earth in many forms, the kingdom of God has already begun and will one day vanquish suffering.

But Jesus didn't trivialize the hurt we feel when we suffer on earth. The night before His crucifixion, Jesus himself lamented His impending torture and death in tears of agony. Having called His closest friends to be there to support Him in His time of trial, Jesus prayed in the garden, "My Father, if it be possible, let this chalice pass from me" (Mt. 26:39). Far from a staid, unquestioning submission to His impending suffering — the crowds' jeers, the whip's sting, the thorns' pricks, and the nails' pangs — Jesus protested this horrible suffering that awaited Him. He was stressed, fearful, and desperate. And in that place of suffering, He asked the Father to spare Him from the evil of death.

The fact that even Jesus was scared to suffer and die shows us that sometimes, it's okay to be afraid. When we face great trials in our lives, we don't always have to be stoically strong. Like Jesus, we can be honest with God by admitting our fear of suffering and asking for help in our time of need. John Paul writes:

> Christ's words confirm with all simplicity this human truth of suffering, to its very depths: suffering is the undergoing of evil before which man shudders. He says: "let it pass from me," just as Christ says in Gethsemane.[105]

In his prayer for deliverance, Jesus evokes the intentions of the entire human community of sufferers who pray to God in hope of receiving grace and deliverance.

Suffering is never easy. It certainly wasn't for Jesus. The Gospel of Luke tells us that Jesus was so tormented the night before His death that "his sweat became like great drops of blood" (22:44). The evangelist paints a vivid picture here to help us understand the agony Jesus felt in the garden as He prepared to die.

Maybe we have been in a similar place before — scared, panicked, abandoned by everyone, and bearing suffering we know we must face alone. In our moments of trial, we can touch that suffering Jesus felt in the garden. Sometimes, though, our anguish gets so bad that God seems far away. Prayer feels impossible. And all we can do is echo Jesus' cry on the Cross: "My God, my God, why have you forsaken me?" (Mt. 27:46)

In making such a prayer, we express the human anguish that often leaves us feeling separated from the goodness of God — an experience that Jesus also shared. And yet these words held a deeper meaning for Jesus, who as the divine Son felt isolated from the Father on Calvary as He carried the weight of the world's sin. The pope explains:

> When Christ says: "My God, My God, why have you abandoned me?" his words are not only an expression of that abandonment which many times found expression in the Old Testament . . . these words on abandonment are born at the level of that inseparable union of the Son with the Father, and are born because the Father "laid on him the iniquity of us all" (Is. 53:6). They also foreshadow the words of Saint Paul: "For our sake he made him to be sin who knew no sin" (2 Cor. 5:21). Together with this horrible weight, *encompassing the "entire" evil of the turning away from God* which is contained in sin, Christ, through the divine depth of his filial union with the Father, perceives in a humanly inexpressible way *this suffering which is the separation,* the rejection *by the Father,* the estrangement from God. But precisely through this suffering he accomplishes the Redemption, and can say as he breathes his last: "It is finished" (Jn. 19:30).[106]

None of us knows what it's like to endure the unspeakable pain Jesus felt as He carried the world's sins on His shoulders on the Cross 2,000 years ago. But we can relate to the loneliness of suffering and the apparent distance it creates between God and us. Jesus' cry on the Cross is the song of lament to which we join our voices when we feel separated from the goodness and love of God in our suffering. In the words of Catholic theologian Gustavo Gutierrez, O.P., Jesus' "cry on the Cross renders more audible and more penetrating the cries of all the Jobs, individuals and collective, of human history." [107]

Ironically, it is when we feel estranged from God in our suffering, when our hearts swell with indignation and lamentations pour from our mouths, that we draw close to God in the crucified Jesus. Our faith in the mystery of the Incarnation refracts our vision to see the Cross as not just another tragedy of a man being unjustly put to death, but the Creator of the universe carrying our sin and sharing fully in our experience of pain. According to John Paul, it is precisely through this experience of suffering on the Cross that Jesus accomplishes our redemption and gives meaning to human suffering:

> Human suffering has reached its culmination in the Passion of Christ. And at the same time, it has entered into a completely new dimension and a new order: *it has been liked to love*, . . . to that love which creates good, drawing it out by means of suffering, just as the supreme good of the Redemption of the world was drawn from the cross of Christ . . . The cross of Christ has become a source from which flow rivers of living water. In it we must also pose anew the question about the meaning of suffering, and read in it, to its very depths, the answer to this question. [108]

Jesus has lifted suffering up from the cold, dark pit of evil into the realm of God's fiery love — compassionate, engaged, and committed — which draws supreme good from evil. This love becomes the source of hope that our journey of faith leads not to suffering, but to paradise. It evokes thanksgiving for our salvation, for which Jesus freely humbled himself and gave everything. And it comforts us in our loneliness, with the assurance that Jesus suffers with us and understands our pain because He has been there before.

John Paul encourages us to receive faith's assurance that although suffering is a mysterious evil we wish we could avoid, God loves us and stands on our side. This is the good news of Jesus, God with us, who saves us from death, who feels our pain, and who walks with us through the dark valley of tears on our sojourn toward heaven.

LESSON 5

Jesus Gives Pain Purpose

Two of the people I have come to admire most are my Grandma and Grandpa Geroulis. I hold them in such high esteem not only for the love they always showered upon me and the rest of our family over the years, but for their courageous perseverance in the midst of great suffering.

Looking back on the last decade, I can't help but cringe at how ferociously suffering took over their lives. Hospital stays became routine for them in order to treat a variety of maladies. Congestive heart failure led both Gram and Gramps into the operating room to undergo painful bypass surgeries, followed by pacemaker implants years later. More suffering came for Gramps in the form of prostate cancer, knee replacement surgery, and severe blood infections, while Gram found herself in the hospital for weeks at a time to battle bronchitis and kidney failure. Gram and Gramps certainly got to know suffering intimately through lots of firsthand experience.

I first realized just how big a part suffering played in their lives in the winter and spring of 2006. Gram had been hospitalized again because her kidneys were failing, and the prognosis was not good. Her body was filling up with fluid, and because of her weak heart, she wasn't a candidate for dialysis. According to Gram's doctors, she had only a matter of months to live. She was allowed to return home but required round-the-clock care — something my Gramps didn't have the physical capability to offer, as he struggled with his own health problems.

My mom, who lived with my grandparents, assumed the role of Gram's primary caregiver during the mornings, evenings, and weekends. But Gram and Gramps needed some extra help while Mom was at work during the day, so I had the privilege of going over to my grandparents' house to lend a hand in the afternoons during the five months leading up to Gram's death. My time with them was truly an education in the school of suffering.

The lessons were difficult to watch. Both Gram and Gramps were in a tremendous amount of physical and spiritual pain on a daily basis. The arthritis covering Gramps' spine and knees caused him excruciating pain when he tried to get up from a sitting position or walk. He often voiced his frustration about being confined to his recliner when he really wanted to be fixing something or working outside in the yard — his two favorite hobbies.

But Gramps still kept fighting for his autonomy. Instead of giving up, he would endure the agony of pulling himself out of his chair and hobble over to his motorized scooter, which he used to cruise around the house. On the scooter he would make himself meals, take out the trash, and even do the laundry. His will to keep moving forward despite his suffering amazed me. Gramps also lived for his afternoon drives when he would run errands and go over to my uncles' auto body shop. Getting out and about always boosted his spirits. And yet there were many days when he didn't feel up to leaving the house and was forced to watch the long hours go by from his chair. There, all he could do was worry about my Gram, his soul mate, and how he would ever get by without her if she died.

While Gramps' poor quality of life remained relatively steady during those six months that I cared for them, Gram's lifestyle gradually diminished with each day. When I first began visiting the house, she was still getting around fairly well with a walker, and her pain was manageable. I would help her to the kitchen where we would sit for hours talking. She loved to reminisce about her youth, and oftentimes Gramps would chime in with stories about when they were dating.

But as the months passed, Gram's mobility lessened and her suffering intensified. With the coming of spring flowers, Gram found herself confined to her bed, which we moved to the living room so she could watch television there. Day by day, her body continued to swell with fluid and just started to shut down. She lost the use of her legs entirely, she could no longer taste the food that she loved, her appetite vanished, and she began to live in a world defined by horrific pain in her back and legs. Gram was so miserable that the only way she could find some peace was in sleep, and that didn't come easily.

At this point, Gram's life, much like Job's, was completely defined by anguish, and it became clear to her that her death was near. She loved Gramps and her family passionately and didn't want to leave us. At the same time, she regretted that she required so much care from her family and worried about being a burden. Knowing she was dying, she also lamented that she wouldn't get a chance to develop a relationship with our daughter, Elizabeth, her great-granddaughter, who was a newborn at the time.

Gram shared these feelings with me during our afternoon conversations, which we had almost every day. But as her body weakened, her voice grew quieter to the point of silence. Morphine helped ease her pain and caused her to sleep most of the day. During the few moments of consciousness she would have, she would ask for water or for her pillows to be adjusted. As her condition worsened, though, she began to make one additional request during these brief awakenings. She asked us to do the unthinkable — to pray for her death.

For about the last two weeks of Gram's life, I sat in my grandparents' living room during the afternoons and spent most of my time watching them both sleep — Gram in her bed and Gramps in his chair. With the breathing sounds of Gram's oxygen pump filling the air, I couldn't help but wonder what it must be like to be them — Gram facing the imminence of death in a drugged stupor and Gramps enduring his own pain while already grieving the loss of his beloved wife and best friend.

Above the bed where my Gram slept hung three photographs that told a much different story than the one they were living: a handsome photo of Gramps in his army uniform, a portrait of Gram smiling as a beautiful young woman in her twenties, and in the middle, a photo of my grandparents dancing cheek-to-cheek on their wedding day. They looked so happy, healthy, and vibrant — images that sharply contrasted with the reality I saw in front of me.

The charming couple who once danced the night away to their favorite big band ballads, who basked in the beauty of nature while cultivating their garden, and who sought the thrills of amusement park rides, could no longer do the things that they loved because of their bodily afflictions. Back then, I thought, Gram and Gramps probably didn't think things would get so bad in their older years. I don't think any of us do.

This is suffering that I, as a fairly healthy young man, know nothing about. At the same time, I can see myself in my grandparents' experiences because I know that their story is one that I will also share. We all must suffer in this life, and this includes the gradual decline in health that comes with aging and eventually dying.

When I looked at the uphill battle Gram and Gramps had to fight on daily basis, it all seemed so meaningless and wasteful. Passion and vibrancy enlivened their hearts during their older years but was always stifled by their physical limitations. But this, unfortunately, is the way suffering works. It stands as an obstacle to our hopes and dreams by preventing us from engaging in the basic activities that make us feel truly alive.

When we want to speed up and fly, suffering puts the brakes on, and we sink into a quicksand of pain which feels counterproductive and senseless.

Doing Good by Suffering

With suffering, there are no escape clauses. Its sharp tendrils reach all of us and cut deeply. But what if we could turn the tables on suffering — not by eliminating our pain altogether but by doing something to give it purpose and meaning? What if we could do good *through* our suffering? According to John Paul, that is precisely what our relationship with Jesus Christ empowers us to do.

We discover this profound truth in what the pope calls the Gospel, or "good news," of suffering. The pope explains that Jesus is the author of this Gospel, which the Church has handed down from its earliest days:

> The witnesses of the Cross and Resurrection of Christ have handed on to the Church and to mankind a specific Gospel of suffering. The Redeemer himself wrote this Gospel, above all by his own suffering accepted in love, so that man "should not perish but have eternal life." This suffering, together with the living word of his teaching, became a rich source for all those who shared in Jesus' sufferings among the first generation of his disciples and confessors and among those who have come after them down the centuries.[109]

Obviously, Jesus didn't write the Gospel of suffering literally by putting quill to paper, as did the evangelists of the four canonical Gospels. But in His words and deeds recorded in Scripture, and passed on via the living Tradition of the Church,

Jesus taught His disciples that their suffering, both individually and collectively, could be a part of His saving ministry. John Paul explains:

> The Gospel of suffering signifies not only the presence of suffering in the Gospel, as one of the themes of the Good News, but also the revelation of the salvific power and salvific significance of suffering in Christ's messianic mission, and subsequently, in the mission and vocation of the Church.[110]

While this Gospel of suffering was first written two millennia ago, two main chapters revealed in its pages tell us how we can continue to do good by our suffering right here, right now: (1) suffering *for* Jesus and (2) suffering *with* Jesus.

1. Suffering for Jesus

The first chapter in the Gospel of suffering is the deliberate decision to endure suffering for the sake of Jesus. In his public ministry, Jesus minced no words about the fact that anyone who participated in His ministry of building God's kingdom would face opposition of the worst kind: "If any man would come after me, let him deny himself and take up his cross and follow me" (Mt. 16:24; Mk. 8:34). He also spoke these unsettling words to His disciples:

> "They will lay their hands on you and persecute you, delivering you up to the synagogues and prisons, and you will be brought before kings and governors for my name's sake. . . . You will be delivered up even by parents and brothers and kinsmen and friends, and some of you they will put to death; you will be hated by all for my name's sake."
>
> —LK. 21:12, 16

I can only imagine the gargantuan leap of faith those first disciples must have made to follow Jesus after hearing this kind of gruesome prediction. Jesus had no doubts about the violent response His ministry would provoke from those in power.

Consequently, fellowship with Jesus required a willingness to endure the severest form of capital punishment in first-century Palestine — crucifixion. This is what Jesus meant when He challenged would-be disciples to "take up your cross." An analogous message today might be "strap yourself to your electric chair." And yet, persecution drew Jesus' disciples into greater conformity to their Lord, who also suffered for the sake of the Gospel. To suffer for Jesus, according to John Paul, was "*particular proof* of likeness to Christ and union with him."[111]

Jesus made it clear that the fainthearted need not apply for any disciple positions in the Christian enterprise. I wonder how I might have reacted if I had been among the original hearers of Jesus' warning: "If they persecuted me they will persecute you" (Jn. 15:30). If Jesus had stopped there, I probably would have gone about my business and disregarded the message of this itinerant preacher of gloom and doom. But the conclusion of this promise would have certainly grabbed my attention: "But not a hair of your head will perish. By your endurance you will gain your lives" (Lk. 21:19).

Characteristic of His rhetorical style, Jesus embedded the message of salvation within a teaching riddle — life lost on earth for his sake will result in eternal life gained: "He who finds his life will lose it, and he who loses his life for my sake will find it" (Mt. 10:39). Suffering and dying for Jesus opens a door through which the persecuted disciple passes into a new life where suffering no longer exists.

When push came to shove, however, the first disciples weren't completely sold on this idea. The jump from reason to faith was too long to make. When accused of being associated with Jesus at the time of His arrest and passion, Peter denied knowing Him three times. Meanwhile, the other disciples went into hiding. The fear of suffering in this world overshadowed the hidden life that Jesus promised.

But upon seeing the risen Lord, the disciples' paralyzing fear was turned inside out as they witnessed with their own eyes that earthly suffering is surmountable. By rising from the dead after a brutal and shameful death, Jesus proved the veracity of His promise — a glorified life awaits those who suffer for His cause. Jesus gave these words of assurance: "In the world you have tribulation; but be of good cheer, I have overcome the world" (Jn. 16:33).

Encountering Jesus' glorified body that once hung beaten and lifeless on the Cross fostered hope for the first Christians that they, too, would be victors over the powers of sin and death. Perhaps none of Jesus' followers experienced a more dramatic change of heart about this truth than the apostle Peter, who wrote in his later ministry:

> Rejoice in so far as you share Christ's sufferings, that you may also rejoice and be glad when his glory is revealed.
>
> — 1 Pet. 4:13

Having experienced the risen Lord, Peter, along with many other disciples, found strength and courage in the power of the Resurrection. They embraced suffering as they continued the work that Jesus began. John Paul explains:

> This first chapter of the Gospel of suffering, which speaks of persecutions, namely of tribulations experienced because of Christ, contains in itself *a special call to courage and fortitude,* sustained by the eloquence of the Resurrection. Christ has overcome the world definitively by his Resurrec-

tion. Yet, because of the relationship between the Resurrection and his Passion and death, he has at the same time overcome the world by his suffering. Yes, suffering has been singularly present in that victory over the world which was manifested in the Resurrection. Christ retains in his risen body the marks of the wounds of the Cross in his hands, feet and side. Through the Resurrection, he manifests *the victorious power of suffering,* and he wishes to imbue with the conviction of this power the hearts of those whom he chose as Apostles and those whom he continually chooses and sends forth.[112]

Many of the first Christians were tortured and sacrificed their lives to spread the Gospel because they believed that by suffering for Jesus, they too would share in the victory of His Resurrection. Only within this context of Easter faith could Jesus' prophecy that all Christians must endure persecution, later echoed by St. Paul (cf. 2 Tim. 3:12), have been met with hope and courage versus despair and apostasy.

Paul, along with Peter and multitudes of early disciples, had their blood spilled at the hands of Roman emperors intent on stamping out the Christian movement. Paul gave his neck to the sword because of his fidelity to Jesus; Peter, deeming himself unworthy to suffer death in the same manner as his Lord, was crucified upside down. As for the other apostles, the majority faced a similar fate. All were martyred but John, who faced martyrdom but miraculously escaped. Countless more martyrs have followed throughout the ages, as history confirms the timeless authenticity of Jesus' promise of persecution.

Yet what is striking is the conviction with which Christians have unflinchingly walked toward suffering and death for Jesus' sake. It is as though they are fearless, and in some cases, consider suffering for Jesus a privilege. Reflecting this spirit is St.

Ignatius, bishop of Antioch, who lived at the turn of the first century A.D.

The Roman Emperor Trajan sentenced Ignatius to be executed by the lions in Rome's arena. The charge — Ignatius was a Christian who refused to offer sacrifice to the Roman gods and incited others to follow his example. En route from Antioch to his execution in Rome, Ignatius wrote seven letters to the local Christian churches. His message exhorted Christians to respect their bishops as God's appointed shepherds and expressed his joy in being given the opportunity to suffer martyrdom for Jesus.

The strongest testimony of Ignatius' desire to suffer for our Lord comes in his letter to the Romans. On his way to battle the beasts in Rome, he anticipated that the Christian community there would be doing everything in their power to liberate him upon his arrival. The prospect of freedom would have been a great source of hope for most unjustly convicted felons like Ignatius, so we might expect his letter to the Roman community to encourage their desire and efforts to vindicate him. But instead, Ignatius wrote just the opposite:

> I look forward with joy to the wild animals held in readiness for me, and I pray that they may attack me; I will coax them to devour me, so that they may not, as happened in some cases, shrink from seizing me . . . [113]

> I am writing to all the Churches and I enjoin all, that I am dying willingly for God's sake, if only you do not prevent it. I beg of you, do not do me an untimely kindness. Allow me to be eaten by the beasts, which are my way of reaching to God. I am God's wheat, and I am to be ground by the teeth of wild beasts, so that I may become the pure bread of Christ.[114]

Who can read these words from Ignatius without marveling at his almost unbelievable confidence in the face of horrific pain and death? Ignatius was so steadfast in Jesus' promise of eternal life and resurrection that even the prospect of being lion food didn't shake his resolve. His hope proved stronger than fear in a life-threatening situation that would have driven many to recant and worship the Roman gods. Ignatius took courage in Jesus' promise:

> "Do not fear those who kill the body but cannot kill the soul. . . . every one who acknowledges me before men, I also will acknowledge before my Father who is in heaven."
> — Mt. 10:28, 32

Like Ignatius, men and women continue to serve God even at the cost of their lives. But ironically, the persecution that often accompanies a lived expression of faith isn't enough to drive everyone away from Jesus and his Church. Instead, the public witness of the martyrs that the Gospel is worth dying for has become a magnetic force that draws new members into the Body of Christ. The second-century Church Father, Tertullian, wrote that the blood of the martyrs is a great source of life from which Christianity grows. In his words, "Afflict us, torment us, crucify us — in proportion as we are mowed down, we increase; the blood of Christians is a seed."[115]

The mission of the apostles to baptize and make disciples of all nations has given birth to the world's largest religion, with 2.1 billion members worldwide. Yet it is a Church that continues to draw massive amounts of persecution. In his apostolic letter, *Tertio Millennio Adveniente*, written for the 2000 Jubilee Year, John Paul comments:

> At the end of the second millennium, the church has once
> again become a church of martyrs. The persecution of
> believers — priests, religious, and laity — has caused a
> great sowing of martyrdom in different parts of the
> world. . . . *This witness must not be forgotten.*[116]

The last century has seen more Christians persecuted and
martyred than any other epoch in history. Some will be forever
etched in the history books: St. Maximilian Kolbe, a Polish priest
who gave up his life in place of another prisoner at Auschwitz in
1941; Dietrich Bonhoeffer, a Lutheran pastor and theologian
killed by the Nazis in 1945; Martin Luther King, a civil rights
activist and Baptist minister assassinated in 1968; and Roman
Catholic Archbishop Oscar Romero, a champion of the poor in
El Salvador, assassinated in 1980. However, the heroic stories of
the majority of martyrs will go forever unmentioned, their witness hidden to the eyes of those who would retell it.

In May of 2000, John Paul led a ceremony called the Ecu-
menical Commemoration of the Witnesses to the Faith of the
20th Century, which was held in the Roman Colosseum — the
place where the blood of countless Christians has been shed.
Those gathered remembered over 10,000 Christians persecuted
and killed on account of their faith. Inspiring stories were told:
a seminarian in Burundi who was fatally wounded in a 1997
massacre that also claimed the lives of forty-four of his class-
mates; a Jesuit priest who was imprisoned and tortured for sev-
enteen years in Albania before his death; and a Chinese
catechist who spent twenty years in prison camps after being
arrested in 1958, when he was only twenty-two.

In *Their Blood Cries Out,* Paul Marshal provides a startling
account of the mass Christian persecution that still exists in
the modern era. According to Marshal, 200 million Christians
in more than 60 countries are now being abused, arrested, tor-

tured, or executed because of their faith. [117] To call yourself a follower of Jesus amid hostile anti-Christians demands much more than reciting creedal formulas and assenting to doctrines. It means putting your life on the line at the hands of those who will willingly take it.

As I reflect on such harsh realities of the modern world, I see a wide chasm between my experience and that of persecuted Christians. Residing in the Midwestern part of the United States, my family and I enjoy the privilege of religious liberty. We worship freely and publicly without barriers of any kind. Never have I been the victim of abuse because of my Christian identity, and I can count on one hand the number of times anyone has ever criticized me because of it. I live in a much different world than the scores of tormented Christians.

My brothers and sisters in Christ who faithfully serve the Lord in the midst of persecution move my heart to pray for their protection and strengthen my resolve to live entirely for God in my own circumstances. They fortify my conviction to bear witness to the Gospel by giving my life to God's purposes. For me, this means courageously persevering in the physical and moral struggles that come with trying to put on Christ in my diverse roles as husband, father, son, brother, friend, writer, and citizen. I know that such an attempt to open myself to God's ways, as Jesus tells us, will always be met with resistance and suffering — albeit a more peaceful suffering than victims of religious persecution endure.

If suffering is the consequence of being a fully-alive Christian, then our greatest consolation and hope comes from the resurrected Jesus. Our union with Jesus' crucified and risen body engrafts us not only into the suffering of the Cross but also into the vindication and glory of the resurrection. We have great reason for hope, as St. Paul reminds us:

> For if we have been united with him in a death like his, we
> shall certainly be united with him in a resurrection like his.
> — Rom. 6:5

According to Jesus, suffering for His sake is our Christian vocation as members of His Body. But John Paul reminds us that, through this darkness, we discover not a dead end but a window to a life where the glory of resurrection awaits. The pope writes:

> To the prospect of the Kingdom of God is linked hope in
> that glory which has its beginning in the Cross of Christ.
> The Resurrection revealed this glory — eschatological
> glory.... Those who share in the sufferings of Christ are also
> called, through their own sufferings, to share in *glory*.[118]

Trusting that our risen Savior reveals to us our destiny, we see suffering as the fire we must pass through in our own transfiguration. We are transients, groaning through the trials of suffering for the Gospel, en route to our final destination where glory awaits us.

One of my grade school teachers offered this reflection to help students envision the future glory:

> Imagine or remember your most joyful day on earth, a day
> that surpasses every other. Then multiply the intensity of
> that joy times a million. Then you will have a glimpse of
> what heaven will be like.

I think my teacher's catechesis echoes the hope of St. Paul who wrote, "For this slight momentary affliction is preparing us for an eternal weight of glory beyond all comparison" (1 Cor. 4:17).

2. Suffering with Jesus

While the Gospel of suffering allows us to transform our suffering into something good by enduring trials for the sake of Jesus, it also reveals a second way — suffering in union with Jesus. According to John Paul, Jesus invites us to partake in His suffering:

> "Follow me! Come! Take part through your suffering in this work of saving the world, a salvation achieved through my suffering! Through my Cross."[119]

This powerful message points to the great mystery of faith that we can join our suffering to Jesus' saving passion and death.

According to the pope, this sharing of suffering is possible only because Jesus engrafts us into His Body — a reality that becomes actualized in a special way through our regeneration in Baptism and our reception of Jesus in the Eucharist. John Paul writes:

> . . . in the act of Baptism, which brings about a configuration with Christ, and then through his Sacrifice — sacramentally through the Eucharist — the Church is continually being built up spiritually as the Body of Christ. In this Body, Christ wishes to be united with every individual, and in a special way he is united with those who suffer.[120]

Here, the pope explains that because Jesus truly lives in us, we can share in His suffering — a truth about which St. Paul expressed his conviction:

> I have been crucified with Christ, it is no longer I who live, but Christ who lives in me: and the life I now live in the

flesh I live by faith in the Son of God, who loved me and
gave himself for me.

— GAL. 2:20

Reflecting on this passage from the apostle Paul, John Paul
writes:

Faith enables the author of these words to know that love
which led Christ to the Cross. And if he loved us in this
way, suffering and dying, then with this suffering and death
of his he lives in the one whom he loved in this way.[121]

In other words, the Body of Christ is no spiritual metaphor
but is comprised of real living persons — Jesus Christ, the Son
of God made man, and the rest of us who have come to share
in His life through grace. In Christ's Body, heaven and earth
meet, as the Son of God himself enters the soul of each one of
us, renews us with His love, and knits us together into the fabric of his Church. It is within this communion of life and love
that Jesus' suffering and ours become one.

To suffer with Jesus as members of His Body is not merely
possible for us as Christians, but it is our vocation within God's
plan of salvation. In the words of John Paul:

The Redeemer suffered in place of man for man. Every man
has his own share in the Redemption. Each one is also
called to share in that suffering through which the Redemption was accomplished. [122]

The pope's teaching that we as individual Christians have
a role to play in redemption through our own suffering probably sounds at least radical, if not downright odd. It's not really
a popular topic broached at the pulpit, nor does it make for

comfortable dinner conversation. It's even a kind of taboo topic within Catholic classrooms. Rarely in my twelve years of being catechized in Catholic schools, five years attending a Catholic college, or two years in seminary, have I heard this idea given much attention. So what exactly does the pope mean when he says we must share in the suffering that accomplished our redemption? [123]

John Paul bases his teaching on the wisdom of Catholic tradition, rooted in a careful reading of St. Paul, who says that our suffering — when joined to the redemptive suffering of Jesus — can become productive and useful. The apostle writes:

> Now I rejoice in my sufferings for your sake, and in my flesh I complete what is lacking in Christ's afflictions for the sake of his body, that is, the Church.
>
> — COL. 1:24

Reflecting on this passage, the pope says that Paul expresses the "exceptional nature" of the union between Jesus and the individual Christian sufferer.[124]

> For, *whoever suffers in union with Christ* . . . "completes" by his suffering "what is lacking in Christ's afflictions."[125]

But what could possibly be lacking in Jesus' afflictions? After all, it's a dogma of the Church that our redemption has been totally accomplished by Jesus' saving passion and death.

Paul's language, "to complete what is lacking," can be confusing because it seems to imply that something is missing from Jesus' redemptive work on the Cross, or that an extra piece needs to be added in order to make it whole. Understood in this erroneous context, the teaching would challenge the fundamental Christian conviction that Jesus' death on the Cross sufficiently atoned for our sins once and for all. But according to John Paul, we can affirm both the sufficiency of Jesus' redemptive work and our own vocation to participate in it. The pope explains:

> The suffering of Christ created the good of the world's redemption. This good in itself is inexhaustible and infinite. No man can add anything to it. But at the same time, in the mystery of the Church as his Body, Christ has in a sense opened his own redemptive suffering to all human suffering. In so far as man becomes a sharer in Christ's sufferings — in any part of the world and at any time in history — to that extent he in his own way completes the suffering through which Christ accomplished the Redemption of the world.
>
> Does this mean that the Redemption achieved by Christ is not complete? No. It only means that the Redemption, accomplished through satisfactory love, *remains always open to all love* expressed in *human suffering*. In this dimension — the dimension of love — the Redemption which has already been completely accomplished is, in a certain sense, constantly being accomplished. Christ achieved the Redemption completely and to the very limits but at the same time he did not bring it to a close. In this redemptive suffering, through which the Redemption of the world was accomplished, Christ opened himself from the beginning to every human suffering and constantly does so. Yes, it seems to be part *of the very essence of Christ's redemptive suffering* that this suffering requires to be unceasingly completed.[126]

John Paul tells us that in one sense, Jesus' redemptive suffering is history — it occurred over two millennia ago in

Jerusalem, when His executioners tortured His physical body. We certainly can't complete what is lacking in Jesus' suffering by going back in a time machine and mounting the Cross with him. That historical event fully paid the price for our sins — nothing can be added to it. Such is the truth given to us in Jesus' own conclusion on the Cross that "It is finished" (Jn. 19:20).

But because Jesus is God, His redemptive suffering has an eternal dimension. According to the pope:

> [Jesus' redemptive work] lives on in the history of man. It lives and develops as the body of Christ, and in this dimension every human suffering, by reason of the loving union with Christ, completes the suffering of Christ.[127]

The mystery of the Church, as "the body which completes in itself also Christ's crucified and risen body . . ." provides the "space or context in which human sufferings complete the sufferings of Christ."[128]

So within the Church, Jesus has infused suffering with a renewed and redemptive meaning. This was Paul's conviction when he claimed to complete what was lacking in the sufferings of Christ on behalf of the Church. Paul was convinced that the trials and persecution he endured during his ministry were not meaningless, but joined to Jesus, they became something more.

Drawing upon this idea, John Paul writes that all human suffering within the Body of Christ possesses a "creative character"[129] in the sense that our suffering, joined to the redemptive power of Jesus' suffering, can be an instrument of good in God's economy of grace. In other words, the union between our pain and the suffering of Jesus, which merited our salvation, can create an opportunity for God to bestow blessings on ourselves and others — a mystery that the Church has traditionally called "redemptive suffering."

The pope reminds us that what was true for Paul two millennia ago remains true for us today. Shining as a beacon for all who fall into the abyss of suffering is the assurance that we can do good by it. At the same time, to say that we have a vocation to share in Jesus' redemptive suffering means that we have a responsibility to suffer well. We do this as members of the Church by joining our suffering to the Cross, as a sacrificial offering of love to God.

Mary, a Catholic mom who lives with her husband, Tom, and their six children in the suburbs of Chicago, tries to put these teachings about suffering into practice amid the chaotic moments of family life. Mary's kids, like most, frequently skin elbows and bonk heads as they play in the yard. And you can often see their busy mom dashing outside to play nurse. As she comforts her children, though, Mary brings her faith in the power of redemptive suffering into play by encouraging her older kids, "Offer it up, offer it up." Sometimes, this little saying can even be heard in a loud voice coming from within the house walls when the children protest their daily chores.

Jim and Kay, a retired couple who lives next door to Mary and her family, have seen her in action. They enjoy sipping iced teas during the spring and summer months on their front porch and are the eyes and ears of the neighborhood. As the couple takes in all of the activity on the block, they often marvel at the extraordinary powers of the "supermom" living next door.

One day as the couple set out for their traditional morning walk, they crossed paths with Mary. After exchanging greetings, Jim inquired, "You know, we have been neighbors for years, and I've just got to ask you a question about a phrase I hear you using all the time."

"Sure, Jim," Mary said. "What phrase is that?"

"Why is it that every time one of your kids hurts themselves or complain you tell them to 'cough it up, cough it up' when they aren't even choking?"

Mary chuckled. "Jim, I'm afraid you misunderstood me," she replied. "I was saying 'offer it up' to encourage the children to offer their suffering in union with the Cross of Jesus Christ. We believe that God can use our sufferings for good."

Offering up our pain, like Mary encouraged her kids to do, is an act of hope in the good news that Jesus enables us to do something positive with our suffering. United to Jesus, whose redemptive suffering was an act of God's saving love and from which grace now overflows, our suffering can become an expression of love and a powerful conduit of God's blessings.

According to the pope, when we embrace our suffering with the "spirit of Christ's sacrifice," it bears the fruits of redemption and becomes an "irreplaceable mediator and author of the good things which are indispensable for the world's salvation." [130] The pope goes on to say that suffering "clears the way for the grace which transforms human souls" and can become an "irreplaceable service" for our brothers and sisters.[131] Theologian Hans Urs von Balthasar illuminates John Paul's teaching with these inspiring words:

> Even suffering, *particularly* suffering, is a precious gift that the one suffering can hand on to others; it helps, it purifies, it atones, it communicates divine graces. The sufferings of a mother can bring a wayward son back to the right path; the sufferings of someone with cancer or leprosy, if offered to God, can be a capital for God to use, bearing fruit in the most unexpected places. Suffering, accepted with thankfulness and handed on, participates in the great fruitfulness of everything that streams from God's joy and returns to him by circuitous paths.[132]

Recently, I went to my local parish church to participate in the Sacrament of Reconciliation. After I confessed my sins to the priest, we discussed one particular sin that I was habitually struggling to remove from my life. I shared with him how it seemed like I had confessed that sin a million times. But no matter how hard I fought to stamp it out, the sin always seemed to creep back into my daily routine.

After empathizing with my predicament, Father gave me a revolutionary strategy for overcoming this sin. He said that the battle itself could be transformed into an act of love if I unite my self-sacrifice to the redemptive Cross of Jesus. Knowing that my wife and I were expecting a new baby girl at the time, he suggested that I offer my moral struggle in union with Jesus' suffering for a very specific intention — the good health of our baby. By virtue of the mystery of redemptive suffering within the Body of Christ, my sacrificial offering to shun sin could benefit our little girl.

With the assurance that my own suffering could become a channel through which God could bless our baby, I started to strive for holiness with greater fervor, patience, and discipline. When the temptation of this sin presented itself, I knew I could pray to Jesus, "Lord, I consecrate all of the frustration and sadness that I bear in my struggle to overcome this sin to you, in union with your saving Cross, for the benefit of my daughter." In that prayer, I received consolation and strength, knowing that my pain became an efficacious sign of love that opened a window through which God's gifts could reach our baby girl.

God extends an invitation to transform our suffering into a catalyst of grace to all members of the Church. Whatever form our pain takes, we can lift it up into the Divine Potter's hands to shape and use for His good purposes. In this act of consecration, says John Paul, we find the meaning of our suffering, and in doing so, the unexpected surprise of joy. The pope writes:

> Gradually, *as the individual takes up his cross,* spiritually uniting himself to the Cross of Christ, the salvific meaning of suffering is revealed before him. He does not discover this meaning at his own human level, but at the level of the suffering of Christ. At the same time, however, from this level of Christ the salvific meaning of suffering *descends to man's level* and becomes, in a sense, the individual's personal response. It is then that man finds in his suffering interior peace and even spiritual joy.[133]

Here, John Paul teaches us that we experience joy in our suffering by discovering its saving meaning, which Jesus gives to us in His call to participate in his Cross.[134] In doing so, the pope assures us that we can overcome the emotions of sadness and despair wrapped up in feeling that we are useless and a burden to others.[135] He writes:

> The discovery of the salvific meaning of suffering in union with Christ transforms this depressing feeling.[136]

Jesus transmutes our suffering into joy; the saving light He casts on the meaning of suffering creates a deep and abiding happiness in us as we come to know that we do not suffer in vain — we suffer in love. Consequently, we begin to share in the joy of which Paul wrote: "I rejoice in my sufferings for your sake" (Col. 1:24). Here, the apostle doesn't describe a masochistic pleasure that delights in pain and seeks suffering for its own sake. He speaks of joy which blossoms from the soul that has achieved its destiny by living and loving in communion with its Lord, who suffers in love.

Such was the experience of St. Thérèse of Lisieux. A Carmelite nun who lived a life marked by pain and obscurity in the cloistered convent of Lisieux, France, Thérèse viewed her own suffering as a ministry. After enduring a serious illness as a young girl that included symptoms of delirium and fainting spells, Thérèse remained frail for the rest of her life. But she was convinced that her suffering could serve others. Thérèse once said, "I prefer the monotony of obscure sacrifice to all ecstasies. To pick up a pin for love can convert a soul."

In her short twenty-four years on earth, Thérèse found in her suffering a sense of joy made known to her by God. During the final months of her life, as she lay dying of tuberculosis, her fellow sisters sat by her bedside and took notes of her last words. In this extract from Mother Agnes' notes, Thérèse talks about how she has discovered happiness in suffering:

> I have found happiness and joy on earth, but solely in suffering, for I've suffered very much here below; you must make it known to souls . . . .
>
> Since my First Communion, since the time I asked Jesus to change all the consolations of this earth into bitterness for me, I had a perpetual desire to suffer. I wasn't thinking, however, of making suffering my joy; this is a grace that was given to me later on. Up until then, it was like a spark hidden beneath the ashes, and like blossoms on a tree that must become fruit in time.[137]

At first reading, these words surprise us. Why would anyone actively desire suffering? The truth is, of course, that Thérèse didn't love suffering. But knowing that her suffering joined to Jesus could benefit souls, she found the secret of suffering well and the joy unexpectedly hidden therein.

When we suffer in union with Jesus, like St. Thérèse did, we enter into the victorious power of the Cross. John Paul writes that in our debility and feebleness, God's strength abounds, "so that every form of suffering, given flesh life by the power of the Cross, should become no longer the weakness of man but the power of God."[138]

As I look back on my personal family history, I see so much weakness wrought by suffering. I remember my dad hooked up to all those hospital machines and barely able to move on his deathbed. I remember my Gram, who lay paralyzed by pain for weeks as she waited for death, and my Gramps, chained to his motorized scooter. I remember my own bouts with sickness and grief that ravaged my body and left me feeling helpless and desperate. And yet the pope and the Church teach us that it is here, in these places of utter uselessness and vulnerability, that the power of God is strongest within us. St. Paul says as much in his message to the Corinthians when he writes, "I will all the more gladly boast of my weaknesses, that the power of Christ may rest upon me" (2 Cor. 12:9).

Blessed Teresa of Calcutta discovered the power of God amid the worst forms of suffering. She founded the Missionaries of Charity in 1950 in order to love those who were hurting. For forty-seven years, she dedicated her life to caring for poor men and women in Calcutta, India — the outcasts, the sick, those who were left to die alone in the gutter. One would think that Mother Teresa's daily experiences of looking into the eyes of those crying out in pain and yearning for deliverance could drag her spirit into the darkness of despair and sadness. How could a person, seeing such concentrated amounts of massive suffering, not conclude that it is all worthless, horrible, and futile?

While Mother Teresa believed that the suffering she encountered was in fact evil, she also recognized how suffering united to Jesus could become an act of love. In her book, *No Greater Love,* she writes:

> Your suffering is a great means of love, if you make use of
> it, especially if you offer it for peace in the world. Suffering
> in and of itself is useless, but suffering that is shared with
> the passion of Christ is a wonderful gift and a sign of
> love.[139]

Faith tells us that our suffering, which appears absurdly
weak in human eyes, can become a strong force of divine communion and grace when we unite it to Jesus. Even if our afflictions impair our physical and mental faculties or render us
completely incapacitated, we can still achieve incredible spiritual productivity. In John Paul's words:

> Faith in sharing in the suffering of Christ brings with it the
> interior certainty that the suffering person "completes what
> is lacking in Christ's afflictions;" the certainty that in the
> spiritual dimension of the work of Redemption he is serv-
> ing, like Christ, the salvation of his brothers and sisters.[140]

We can believe that suffering with Jesus is not wasted existence but serves as an effective offering that God can use for
good.

At the same time, sharing in Jesus' suffering is a struggle. As
we strive to carry the Cross in the midst of our own trials, pain
doesn't cease to hurt us. This is why we must avail ourselves of
the comfort that Jesus wants to give us. St. Paul writes, "For as
we share abundantly in Christ's sufferings, so through Christ
we share abundantly in comfort too" (2 Cor. 1:5).

If we peer deep into the shadows of our suffering through
eyes of faith, we recognize the silhouette of Jesus, who loves us
and draws close to help us in our pain. John Paul writes that in
suffering there is a "concealed power that draws a person inte-
riorly close to Christ, a special grace."[141] It is Jesus, the pope

assures us, who "acts at the heart of human suffering through his Spirit of truth, through the consoling Spirit. It is he who transforms . . . the very substance of the spiritual life, indicating for the person who suffers a place close to himself."[142]

That Jesus draws especially near to us in our suffering can be hard to believe when our pain often leaves us feeling so far away from Him. But John Paul reminds us that although our Lord might seem a thousand miles away when we suffer, He is with us and wraps His arms around us in a holy embrace as His suffering and ours become one. Even more, it is in this communion of suffering with Jesus that He gradually reveals to us "the horizons of the Kingdom of God: the horizons of a world converted to the Creator, of a world free from sin, a world being built on the saving power of love . . ." and leads us into God's kingdom "through the very heart of our suffering."[143]

Suffering is always a shared experience between Jesus and us. In our many trials, Jesus is with us — holding us tight and consoling us amid the afflictions that rack our bodies and souls. He is with us — transforming our tears into joy by the redemptive power of His Cross. He is with us — opening the eyes of our hearts to see the fullness of salvation that awaits us in paradise, where suffering is no more.

Making the Leap of Faith

Believing that suffering can be something good for us, or can do something good for others, requires substantial faith. After all, suffering hurts us, and in most cases, makes us feel terrible — exhausted, nauseated, pained, sad, afraid, confused, frustrated, disappointed, angry, depressed, etc. How counterintuitive it is, then, to think that suffering can be compatible in any way with God and goodness.

As I reflect on the Gospel of suffering, I can't help but wonder, "How does it all work? How do I know it's really true?" It seems impossible.

From there, I find myself backed into a corner. I can both embrace my critical nature and doubt the authenticity of Revelation because it seems so incredibly strange, or I can make the leap of faith across the giant chasm of suspicion. Such is the age-old challenge the Gospel imposes on everyone who hears its message. Even the apostles Peter and Thomas found themselves in this precarious position — divided between human logic and the unfathomable ways of God.

For Peter, a strong gust of wind reminded him of how absurd Jesus' invitation was to step overboard and walk on the turbulent waves of the sea. A fisherman by trade, Peter knew the madness of such a feat. How could he really believe he could do the impossible? Matthew's Gospel tells the story:

> And in the fourth watch of the night he came to them, walking on the sea. But when the disciples saw him walking on the sea, they were terrified, saying, "It is a ghost!" And they cried out for fear. But immediately he spoke to them, saying, "Take heart, it is I; have no fear." And Peter answered him, "Lord, if it is you, bid me come to you on the water." He said, "Come." So Peter got out of the boat and walked on the water and came to Jesus; but when he saw the wind, he was afraid, and beginning to sink he cried out, "Lord, save me." Jesus immediately reached out his hand and caught him, saying to him, "O you of little faith, why did you doubt?" And when they got into the boat, the wind ceased.
>
> — Mt. 14:25-32

Like Peter, Thomas also couldn't bring himself to believe the seemingly impossible. On Sunday evening of that first

Easter, the risen Jesus appeared to the apostles, who out of fear had locked themselves in a hiding place. There, Jesus gave them the gift of the Holy Spirit and sent them forth to continue His mission of preaching the Gospel.

Thomas wasn't there that night. He found out about what happened from the other apostles, who told him, "We have seen the Lord" (Jn. 20:25). But a second-hand account wasn't good enough for Thomas, especially regarding such a huge claim. He said, "Unless I see in his hands the print of the nails, and place my finger in the mark of the nails, and place my hand in his side, I will not believe" (20:25). Thomas needed to see and touch the risen Jesus himself. Despite the reliable testimony of his closest friends, Thomas wanted empirical evidence of Jesus' raised body to prove beyond a doubt that the resurrection was real.

Eight days later, Thomas would get the evidence he needed. The risen Jesus appeared to him and the other apostles again in their place of hiding. Jesus said to Thomas, "Put your finger here, and see my hands; and put out your hand, and place it in my side; do not be faithless, but believing" (20:27). In that moment, Thomas' doubt turned to faith, which prompted him to proclaim Jesus as "My Lord and my God!" (20:28). But Jesus replied, "You have believed because you have seen me. Blessed are those who have not seen and yet believe" (20:29).

Like Peter and Thomas, we all face the same challenge of saying "Amen" to the many mysteries of Revelation we don't fully understand. The Gospel constantly provokes our curiosity and sparks our imagination to envision the power of God doing the seemingly impossible — like supporting Peter on the water, raising Jesus' body from the dead, and drawing good out of our suffering. But faith believes the unbelievable. For it is "the assurance of things hoped for, the conviction of things not seen"(Heb. 11:1).

Faith in the Gospel of suffering empowers our hope with the conviction that we can transcend our many trials and afflictions. It assures us that by suffering for Jesus' sake, we gain our lives. It gives meaning to our anguish which, united to Jesus' saving Cross, can become an act of love that benefits the Church. It comforts us with the confidence that our Lord is intimately close to us in our pain.

All of these truths are invisible to the naked eye. But faith sees them. It knows that, by God's power and love, we can do good by our suffering.

LESSON 6

Suffering Calls Forth Love

Suffering can hurt us. It can pierce our flesh. It can squeeze tears from our eyes. It can rob us of our independence. It can anger us. It can depress us. It can even kill us. Undoubtedly, suffering is a force of evil to be reckoned with in our lives.

But Revelation assures us that suffering can't destroy us. It can't render our lives meaningless. It can't rob us of our hope in the promises of God. Nor can the weakness suffering brings make us helpless in God's economy of grace.

Such convictions of hope become illuminated in Jesus Christ, in whom "the riddles of sorrow and death grow meaningful."[144] God has revealed His magnificent love for us in Jesus, who saved us through suffering and who suffers with us. At the same time, Jesus assures us that our suffering isn't wasted. By the saving power of His passion and death, He has given all who suffer the opportunity to tap the fruits of redemption and cooperate with Him in pouring out divine gifts for the good of the world.

In light of these truths seen through the prism of faith, we can make the amazing and seemingly paradoxical conclusion with the Church that suffering is an evil that has become something good in Christ and can become something good for us. This is, indeed, the good news of suffering.

And yet, as Jesus' disciples, we also hear His call to alleviate suffering with compassionate love. To do so, according to our Lord, is to fulfill our most important purpose in life next to loving God — loving our neighbor. John Paul writes:

Christ's revelation of the salvific meaning of suffering is in no way identified with an attitude of passivity. Completely the reverse is true. The Gospel is the negation of passivity in the face of suffering.[145]

The pope reminds us that while we can think of suffering as something good in the light of faith, we must at the same time do good by helping those who suffer. Love that works to alleviate human hurt defines the Christian response to the suffering of others.

The Good Samaritan

Among Jesus' many parables that emphasize the importance of loving sufferers, the one that most clearly expresses this teaching is the story of the Good Samaritan. According to John Paul, this famous parable "belongs to the Gospel of suffering" and offers us essential insights into the Christian meaning of suffering.[146]

Contained in the pages of Luke's Gospel, the parable comes as Jesus' response to the questions of a scholar of the law, or lawyer, who is skeptical of Jesus' religious knowledge. In order to test Jesus, the lawyer asks a question to see if Jesus will respond correctly. He inquires, "Teacher, what shall I do to inherit eternal life?" (Lk. 10:25)

As we read the narrative, we get the feeling Jesus knows He is being tested, because He refuses to give the lawyer a direct answer. Instead, He tells the lawyer to respond to his own question by consulting the law as it is written in Scripture. By nature of his profession, the lawyer knows the law very well and replies by quoting passages from Dt. 6:5 and Lev. 19:18:

"You shall love the Lord your God with all your heart, and with all your soul, and with all your strength, and with all your mind; and your neighbor as yourself."

— Lk. 10:27

After hearing these scriptural excerpts, Jesus affirms that the lawyer has spoken correctly. Love of God and love of neighbor are the two key moral requirements that anyone who wants to inherit eternal life must fulfill. However, the lawyer wants Jesus to clarify what exactly love of neighbor means and asks: "And who is my neighbor?" (Lk. 10:29). Jesus replies with the parable of the Good Samaritan:

> "A man was going down from Jerusalem to Jericho, and he fell among robbers, who stripped him and beat him, and departed, leaving him half dead. Now by chance a priest was going down that road; and when he saw him he passed by on the other side. So likewise a Levite, when he came to the place and saw him, passed by on the other side. But a Samaritan, as he journeyed, came to where he was; and when he saw him, he had compassion, and went to him and bound up his wounds, pouring on oil and wine; then he set him on his own beast and brought him to an inn, and took care of him. And the next day he took out two denarii and gave them to the innkeeper, saying, 'Take care of him; and whatever more you spend, I will repay you when I come back.' Which of these three, do you think, proved neighbor to the man who fell among the robbers?" He said, "The one who showed mercy on him." And Jesus said to him, "Go and do likewise."
>
> — Lk. 10:30-37

Reflecting on the parable, John Paul writes that Jesus teaches us about the kind of relationship he expects us to have with our suffering neighbors.[147] Like the Good Samaritan, we also must respond with both a compassionate recognition of those who suffer and an active effort to help relieve their pain. In the pope's words, "We are not allowed to 'pass by on the other side' indifferently'"[148] as the priest and Levite did when they saw the suffering man in the road. Rather, Jesus calls us to imitate the Good Samaritan, who made himself available to the suffering man in need of care.

One aspect of the story that John Paul believes to be especially significant is the Samaritan's action of "stopping." Undoubtedly, most of us have a laundry list of to-dos and projects going on at any given moment. I know in my own life as a husband, father, and writer, things seem to get busier with each passing day. On the calendar is a long scribbled list of commitments, the chores around the house just keep mounting, and the in-box on my desk is now overflowing. Such realities of everyday living make "stopping" a formidable challenge — even to help someone in need. However, the pope writes that if we truly hear the voice of our Savior, "we must stop beside" those who suffer.[149]

But how can we stop to help someone we don't even realize is there? Perhaps one of the greatest obstacles to fulfilling our vocation to be Good Samaritans is chronic blindness to others' pain. I frequently notice that, although I go about my business with my eyes wide open, I don't really allow others' suffering to enter into my field of sight. My attention tends to fixate on my world. It's almost as if I contract a kind of tunnel vision. I target my eyes on my own goals and concerns while deliberately keeping everything and everyone else out of focus in my peripheral vision.

Unlike me, the Good Samaritan saw the big picture. He didn't allow his own agenda to get in the way of seeing the wounded man and stopping to help — even though he probably would have been in a hurry, much like the rest of us. After all, the parable says the Samaritan was on a journey, so he would have wanted to get to where he was going in a timely manner. Maybe he was traveling on business and on his way home to see his family, who anxiously awaited his arrival. Or perhaps he was en route to visit friends whom he had not seen for a while. Regardless, the Good Samaritan was going somewhere and charted his course with a specific purpose in mind. Whatever that purpose was, however, he didn't allow it to put restraints on his availability to the suffering man who presented an immediate need.

The Good Samaritan's openness to others is the example Jesus asks us to follow. Our Lord calls us to expand our field of vision beyond ourselves so we can more readily perceive the needs of those around us. According to the pope, becoming a Good Samaritan involves "the opening of a certain interior disposition of the heart" in which we are "moved by the misfortune of another" and sensitive to others' pain.[150] This sensitivity to how others are feeling "bears witness to compassion toward the suffering person"[151] and is the spiritual bedrock of living as Good Samaritans in the world.

The energizing force that prompts us to habitually care for and perceive others' needs is compassion. A term that literally means "to suffer together," compassion is an interior disposition that enables us to "feel into" another's suffering in such a deep way that we identify with their hurt. Sometimes, when confronted with someone else's struggles, we'll say or hear the remark, "I feel your pain." We'll often make such a statement casually, but it still communicates the true essence of compassion: an awakening of sympathy for another person in such a way that two experiences, theirs and ours, become a kind of shared reality. In compassion, says John Paul, we express "our love for and solidarity with the sufferer."[152]

Compassion is the spark that ignites our will to act on behalf of sufferers. The Good Samaritan didn't just feel sorry for the man on the roadside and go about his business; rather, he gave his compassion expression by actively helping to reduce the injured man's suffering. The parable tells us that, upon seeing the man, the Good Samaritan "had compassion and went to him" (Lk 10:33). He tended to the man's wounds with oil and wine, took care of him through the night, and secured a safe place for him to recover at the inn. John Paul elaborates:

> The Good Samaritan of Christ's parable does not stop at sympathy and compassion alone. They become for him an incentive to actions aimed at bringing help to the injured man.[153]

Like the Good Samaritan, we have to take the first step and make our concern for others into a personal mission of mercy. But, as most of us have come to learn, the Good Samaritan's shoes often seem too big to fill.

Eight years ago, on a brisk afternoon in March, I went for a jog in our local park. As I trotted along the running track, the cutest little dog ran up alongside me. Tail wagging and big brown eyes sparkling, she started to jump up and paw at me mid-stride. She was so enthusiastic to see me, I couldn't resist stopping to give her a belly rub.

But upon taking a closer look at my new furry friend, I quickly realized she was neglected. Her ribs pressed through her gaunt torso, dirt covered her matted coat, and her shredded collar hung on by a string. As I examined her, a man who frequented the park shouted to me, "She's been wandering around here for days!" It was obvious the dog was homeless and needed help.

Now what do I do? I thought. I loved dogs. I wanted to take her home, but I didn't have any experience as a dog owner. Plus, I was living with my mom at the time and wasn't sure if she would go for the idea of bringing a dog into the house. But, after some deliberation, I decided to take a risk. I called Mom on her cell phone and explained the situation. After a few minutes of weighing the pros and cons, she agreed.

So I coaxed my new little friend into my car and whisked her away to her new living quarters at our place. The poor thing cried the whole way home and wanted to spend most of the ride on my lap. But the happy ending is that after many bowls of food, a bath, and a trip to the vet, she was good as new. Today, my faithful canine companion, Prinnie, is back to her old healthy self again and a beloved member of the Schroeder family.

Now, every time I hear or read the parable of the Good Samaritan, I think of Prinnie. She gave me the chance to be a Good Samaritan to her. And as I continue my life journey as a Christian, I'm discovering an abundance of opportunities to serve as a minister of compassion in my family, among my friends, and in my community. But I struggle with not letting my own projects and agenda get in the way. For me, self-absorption and busy-ness are the archenemies of the Gospel way of love modeled by the Good Samaritan.

This proved to be true recently on my way home from the grocery. As I was waiting at the traffic light to exit the store parking lot, I saw a young woman standing on the side of the road. Probably in her early thirties, she was attractive, not unkempt or frail, like Prinnie that day in the park. Nor did she bear the wounds of physical abuse, like the man who fell victim to robbers in the parable. She simply held a cardboard sign that, in big black letters, said *Need Help!*

As I looked at the woman, I felt sorry for her. She seemed so lost. Surrounded by what appeared to be a sea of purpose, filled with people rushing around to get things done, she stood still and begged for mercy. The traffic light turned green, and I began to wonder what her story was and how I could help. But, like the many other cars speeding along, I just passed her by. I was on a tight schedule, and my family was expecting me home for dinner. Surely, I didn't have time to stop.

But looking back on the situation, I know I could have stopped. I felt compassion for the woman, but I didn't act on it. Why? Certainly, I could have called Sarah to let her know I would be a little late. If I had explained the situation, she would have understood the reason for my delay. Instead, I ignored the woman's need because I placed greater value on my own agenda and convenience. I was tired and hungry. I wanted to get home to spend time with my family; so I allowed the woman on the side of the road to enter my field of vision and compassion, but I failed to respond with any kind of help.

Being Good Samaritans means putting our compassion into practice by helping those who suffer. According to John Paul, the help we give should be "as far as possible, effective."[154] In other words, the pope says we should strive to fill the needs of those who suffer as best we can. A Good Samaritan is one who offers help with "his whole heart" and doesn't "spare material means."[155]

Applying this lesson to my encounter with the woman who needed help, I realize I could have heeded Jesus' call to "go and do likewise" by giving my compassion hands and feet to bring her aid. If I had stopped, I could have found out what the nature of her need was. Maybe she was homeless, or hungry, or thirsty, or scared, or addicted. If I had taken the time to ask, maybe I could have helped her. I could have bought her dinner at one of the many neighboring restaurants. I could have put her in contact with an outreach center for the homeless in our area. I could have listened and tried to comfort her. I see now that such actions would have expressed the kind love Jesus wants us to give those who suffer in our midst.

The Way to Life

The key message of the Good Samaritan parable is that love is the Christian response to the suffering of others. In this sense, suffering takes on new meaning as an experience of evil that also calls forth human love in the world. The pope writes that suffering is "present to unleash love in the human person, that unselfish gift of one's 'I' on behalf of other people, especially those who suffer."[156] In other words, the world of suffering beckons the creation and sustained existence of another world that is its opposite — the world of love.[157]

According to John Paul, suffering gives us an opportunity to express "that unselfish love" that stirs within us.[158] When we help sufferers, we bring the love of Jesus to those we care for and fulfill our commission to be Good Samaritans in the world. At the same time, the pope teaches us that in this very act of self-donation we find something quite unexpected — ourselves. Drawing from the wisdom of the Second Vatican Council, the pope says that the only way we fully discover who we truly are is by giving ourselves away in love.[159]

Finding who we really are means finding our life in God. And this is the event that happens, according to Jesus, when we reach out in love to our suffering neighbors. For love given freely to others leads to lasting fulfillment and happiness because it unites us to God, who is Love (1 Jn. 4:16), and paves our way to eternal life. On the other hand, withholding love from the sufferers around us is the surest way to become lost. Jesus consistently threads these themes into His preaching, but they are perhaps no more prominent than in the Judgment of Nations discourse (Mt. 25:31-46).

There, Jesus describes the end of time, when He will return to earth to conduct a judgment of all human beings. The narrative uses the imperial imagery of a king, his kingdom, and his subjects to tell us how this judgment will take place. Jesus is the king who, like a shepherd who separates sheep from goats, will separate His subjects (us) into one of two groups — the righteous and the wicked. He will welcome the righteous into the kingdom (eternal life) and will exclude the wicked from the kingdom (eternal punishment). So the stakes couldn't be higher. The outcome of Jesus' judgment will determine where each one of us will spend our eternity.

In any type of activity where an evaluation of our performance is involved, we need to know the criteria the judges will be using so we can tailor our activities and behavior accordingly. If I'm a student writing a paper for school, I need to know the qualities upon which the teacher will base my grade such as content, grammar, spelling, page length, format, etc. If I'm interviewing for a job, I need to know what characteristics the organization believes an employee must have in order to perform well in the position such as industry experience, education, specialized skills, mobility, etc. In the same way, if I want to enter the kingdom of God, I need to know what qualities Jesus deems important for its citizens.

Thankfully, he gives us valuable insights here. Jesus tells us that the righteous and worthy of the kingdom will be those of us who have responded with loving care to the sufferers we encounter during our earthly journey, while the wicked and unworthy of the kingdom will be those who have neglected others in need.

This method of evaluation becomes clear as Jesus describes how he will communicate his verdict. To those who cared for sufferers in this life will come words of welcome and invitation:

> "Come, O blessed of my Father, inherit the kingdom prepared for you from the foundation of the world; for I was hungry and you gave me food, I was thirsty and you gave me drink, I was a stranger and you welcomed me, I was

naked and you clothed me, I was sick and you visited me,
I was in prison and you came to me."

— MT. 25:34-36

But those who neglected others' needs will hear words of
exclusion and condemnation:

> "Depart from me, you cursed, into the eternal fire prepared
> for the devil and his angels; for I was hungry and you gave
> me no food, I was thirsty and you gave me no drink, I was
> a stranger and you did not welcome me, naked and you
> did not clothe me."
>
> — MT. 25:41-43

In the story, Jesus baffles both the righteous and wicked
with the way He ties care for others to care for himself. Members from both groups ask him, "When did we see you? When
did we care for you? When did we not care for you?" And Jesus
answers, "Truly, I say to you, as you did it to one of the least of
these my brethren, you did it to me . . . as you did it not to one
of the least of these, you did it not to me" (Mt. 25:40, 45).

So we come to learn that Jesus' two great commandments
— love of God and love of neighbor — are really inseparable.
They are two sides of the same coin. Every human person bears
Jesus' own face, and in every sufferer we come to know our
suffering Savior. The pope explains:

> Christ said: "You did it to me." He himself is the one who
> in each individual experiences love; he himself is the one
> who receives help . . . He himself is present in this suffering
> person, since his salvific suffering has been opened once
> and for all to every human suffering.[160]

By the power of the Spirit that unites us to Jesus and allows us to participate in His saving Cross, we also come to know Him and serve Him in our suffering neighbors. Blessed Teresa of Calcutta beautifully expresses this conviction in her theology of service to the poor. She writes:

> Jesus is the hungry to be fed.
> Jesus is the thirsty to be satiated.
> Jesus is the naked to be clothed.
> Jesus is the homeless to be taken in.
> Jesus is the sick to be healed.
> Jesus is the lonely to be loved.
> Jesus is the unwanted to be wanted.
> Jesus is the leper to wash His wounds.
> Jesus is the beggar to give Him a smile.
> Jesus is the drunkard to listen to Him.
> Jesus is the mentally ill to protect Him.
> Jesus is the little one to embrace Him.
> Jesus is the blind to lead Him.
> Jesus is the dumb to speak to Him.
> Jesus is the crippled to walk with Him.
> Jesus is the drug addict to befriend Him.
> Jesus is the prostitute to remove from danger and
>   befriend Her.
> Jesus is the prisoner to be visited.
> Jesus is the old to be served.[161]

Here, Mother Teresa shows the clarity of her understanding about Jesus' call to love. To care for others is to care for Jesus and to inherit the joy of eternal life. To neglect others is to neglect Jesus and to lose any hope of happiness. Therefore, it is ironically in keeping all for ourselves that we ultimately lose our lives, and in giving ourselves away to sufferers that we gain everything.

With this truth in mind, John Paul writes:

> Christ's words about the Final Judgment unambiguously show how essential it is, for the eternal life of every individual, to "stop", as the Good Samaritan did, at the suffering of one's neighbor, to have "compassion" for that suffering, and to give some help.[162]

The pope encourages us to listen to the voice of the Good Shepherd, who calls us to life through love.

Am I a Neighbor?

Hearing Jesus' call to love in the Good Samaritan parable and the Judgment of Nations discourse always makes me a little nervous. I think it's because I know I'm not doing as well as I should to see Jesus in others and to respond with compassionate service. If I open my eyes and look beyond myself, I see friends and family members who are struggling and need help. I see my elderly next door neighbor who is homebound and lonely because he never receives any visitors. I see understaffed outreach ministries at church that need volunteers. I see people starving and out of work on the streets of the city. Just in my own little corner of the world, I see hundreds of sufferers, each bearing their own unique wounds on the side of the road.

Suffering confronts all of us every day. So the challenge becomes: How do we help? How do we live as Good Samaritans today — right here, right now, in the world where we live? What are the opportunities? What resources do we need? How have we succeeded in the past? How have we failed? What can we learn from our experiences that will help us become better ministers of Jesus' compassion going forward?

It seems this examination of conscience and spiritual strategizing is the kind of effect Jesus' parables were designed to provoke. They prompt us to take an honest look at ourselves — who we need to be, and where we want to go — and then to evaluate what kind of personal calisthenics we need to do to get ourselves into shape.

In the parable of the Good Samaritan, Jesus switches our attention from discerning "who deserves to be cared for" to "who we are as ones who are called to offer care freely in love." He does this by putting a new twist on the ancient Jewish understanding of "love your neighbor." The lawyer wants Jesus to define "neighbor" in terms of an object of love. "Who is my neighbor?" he asks the Lord, in an attempt to identify which members of society *must* be loved according to the requirements of the law.

But Jesus turns the lawyer's question on its head by presenting an entirely unique notion of neighbor. After telling the parable, Jesus asks the lawyer to identify which among the priest, Levite, and Samaritan proved to "be a neighbor" to the man who fell victim to robbers. In this sense, Jesus uses the term "neighbor" to describe not the recipient of love but the giver of love. According to John Paul, "neighbor" doesn't draw a line in the sand to mark the boundaries of love, but describes the person who loves.[163]

Jesus implies that a better question to ask than "Who is my neighbor?" is "Am I a neighbor?" With this change of emphasis, Jesus lets us know that others are no longer under the microscope — we are. In other words, we need not spend a lot of time distinguishing neighbors (whom we have to love) from nonneighbors (whom we don't have to love), because no distinction exists. Every person is a neighbor who deserves our love, even those who are against us. Jesus makes this point clear:

"You have heard that it was said, 'You shall love your neighbor and hate your enemy.' But I say to you, Love your enemies and pray for those who persecute you."

— MT. 5:43-44

Neighbors never leave anyone standing outside the circle of their love.

Jesus' message sounds radical to our modern ears, but it probably came as an even bigger shock to the lawyer and others who first heard the parable. Jump back 2,000 years to first-century Palestine. Jesus, a Jew, preached the parable of the Good Samaritan to other Jews. How ironic and disturbing, the lawyer and other listeners must have thought, that Jesus made a Samaritan the hero of the story as opposed to the priest and Levite, who were esteemed members of the Jewish community. After all, the notion of a Good Samaritan would have been an oxymoron to a Jewish audience, who considered Samaritans schismatics and enemies. In Jewish circles, to be called a "Samaritan" was an insult. So when the Samaritan appeared on the scene in the parable, everyone listening probably expected him to be the villain rather than the hero.

But Jesus broke new religious ground by inviting the Jewish lawyer to model the Samaritan, who risked much to help the man on the side of the road. Jews didn't associate with Samaritans, nor Samaritans with Jews. But the Good Samaritan put these cultural and religious traditions aside to stop and help the injured man, who was most likely a Jew. Compassion deflated any human prejudices that would have justified the Samaritan's decision to leave the man alone.

Not only did the Samaritan spend time and money to bring aid to the suffering man, but he also risked the religious stigma of defilement associated with touching a dead body. To come into contact with a corpse was to risk being deemed unclean, which resulted in banishment from worship and the community for a time. Upon seeing the man lying still on the side of the road, the Samaritan probably didn't know at that point if the man was alive or dead — an uncertainty that surely complicated his choice about whether to help. And yet the Samaritan acted as a neighbor by giving charity precedence over everything else.

Such is the love of neighbor that leads to eternal life, according to Jesus. It doesn't always accord with conventional attitudes or personal convenience, but requires a total investment of self. It avails itself entirely to those who need our help, and in doing so, serves our Lord himself.

Most of us have come to discover that, while we aspire to be this kind of neighbor, actually doing so is extremely difficult on a daily basis. There is so much suffering and so many who need help in our families, communities, and workplaces. And then there are those who suffer beyond our immediate view — the poor, the sick, the lonely, and the dying throughout the world. Confronting this superabundance of suffering can be overwhelming as we try to figure out where and how to be Good Samaritans with only a limited amount of time and resources. It can leave us paralyzed with uncertainty and asking, "Where do I even start? Will my help really make a difference?"

Once upon a time, there was a wise old man who used to wake early in the morning to read the classics and write poetry by the ocean. Before he would begin his work, he enjoyed strolling along the beach to behold the golden beauty of the sunrise and to feel the refreshing cool mist of the sea on his face. For the old man, it was a time of quiet and solitude, as the beach-goers didn't arrive until later in the morning.

One day on his walk, the old man noticed a silhouette in the distance, a figure moving back and forth from the water's edge. As the old man drew closer, the shape came into focus. It was a boy picking up starfish in the sand and throwing them back into the ocean. The night's tide had washed thousands of them onto the beach.

The old man approached the lad and greeted him, "Good morning!"

"Hi," the boy said, panting as he continued to move feverishly to and fro, picking up starfish and tossing them into the ocean.

"May I ask what you are doing, son?" the old man asked.

"The water brought all of these starfish onto the sand overnight, and they can't return by themselves," replied the boy. "If I leave them here, the sun will cause them all to die. So I'm trying to rescue them by throwing them back into the ocean so they can live."

The old man admired the young man's sensitivity, but he couldn't help but think the boy's efforts to help the starfish seemed futile.

Smiling, the old man said, "Well, that's very kind of you. I'm sure they appreciate it. But son, take a look around. There are miles of beach stretching along the coastline covered with starfish. You'll never be able to get to them all in time. You can't really make a difference, son. Why don't you just have fun and play a while in the sand before the heat of the day sets in?"

The boy bent down, picked up another starfish, and hurled it into the sea. As the starfish met the water, he turned to the old man and replied with a grin, "Well, I made a difference for that one, didn't I?"

One more lesson we can learn from the parable of the Good Samaritan is that loving our neighbors begins with a single step to reach out to those who need us, one by one. At times, we hear the voice of the old man telling us that we can't make a difference when there is so much suffering. But reflecting back on the parable, we see that the Good Samaritan didn't save the world. He reached out to the wounded man he encountered on his particular journey. The Good Samaritan helped who he could, with the resources and time he had, as did the boy who tried to save the starfish.

This is the model that Jesus calls us to follow. He doesn't demand the impossible. He asks each of us to be ministers of loving mercy within the context of our unique vocation and life circumstances. This means that to some degree, even our most radical self-offerings of love will be limited because we exist in time and space. We can't be everywhere, doing everything, to help everyone at once.

However, when we become neighbors of love who minister to sufferers, a kind of ripple effect happens. Our individual work to help those who suffer joins the similar efforts of others in our family, church, community, and throughout the world — the sum total of which brings healing and peace on a much larger scale than we could ever have imagined possible.

Social activist Dorothy Day founded the Catholic Worker Movement based on this principle. Declared a Servant of God by Pope John Paul II (who also opened her cause for sainthood), Day worked for most of her life to serve the poor, for whom she established a nationwide network of hospitality houses. She writes:

> What we would like to do is change the world — make it a little simpler for people to feed, clothe, and shelter themselves as God intended them to do. And to a certain extent, by fighting for better conditions, by crying out unceasingly for the rights of workers, of the poor, of the destitute — the rights of the worthy and the unworthy poor, in other words — we can to a certain extent change the world; we can work for the oasis, the little cell of joy and peace in a harried world. We can throw our pebble in the pond and be

confident that its ever-widening circle will reach around the world.[164]

Dorothy Day believed that even small acts of love can have a global impact. Likewise, John Paul assures us that each act of love we perform for our suffering brothers and sisters is a living stone that helps build a "civilization of love."[165] This is a world community not entirely free from suffering, as that is the human condition, but one that bears witness to the love of God by caring for sufferers, promoting wellness, and alleviating pain in the spirit of the Good Samaritan.

According to the pope, establishing a love-based civilization requires more than our individual efforts added together. It takes the joining of hearts, hands, and minds in communities and institutions dedicated to doing Good Samaritan work on behalf of the suffering. As a people, we can collectively channel our individual responses of mercy in a single direction to become a community of neighbors who work for the benefit of sufferers.

Reflecting on Good Samaritan work in the modern world, John Paul points to the proliferation of helping professions such as doctors, nurses, counselors, teachers, and many others that serve the suffering. This trend, he says, ". . . undoubtedly proves that people today pay ever greater and closer attention to the sufferings of their neighbour, seek to understand those sufferings and deal with them with ever greater skill."[166] Good Samaritan work also continues due to those "devoting to this cause all the time and energy at their disposal outside their professional work."[167] Here, the pope speaks of charitable organizations, apostolates that serve the suffering in communion with the Church, and families that care for their own suffering members and those of other families.

All of us have no doubt been helped by individuals within such groups that make compassion their mission. They have seen Christ in our faces and have given His love to us through their service. Their acts of mercy, no matter how big or small, are working to change the world. According to the pope:

> Thanks to them, the fundamental moral values, such as the value of human solidarity, the value of Christian love of neighbour, form the framework of social life and interhuman relationships and combat on this front the various forms of hatred, violence, cruelty, contempt for others, of simple insensitivity, in other words, indifference toward one's neighbour and his sufferings.[168]

Love given to sufferers is the leaven of society. By following the example of the Good Samaritan, who was sensitive to others' pain and willing to respond with compassion, we can transform not only individual lives but entire cultures.

However, the reverse is also true. All we need to do is look at the horrors of war, poverty, slavery, racism, and genocidal madness that mark our past and present to see what insensitivity to others' suffering looks like. For these reasons, John Paul emphasizes "the enormous *importance of having the right attitudes in education.*"[169]

To a large degree, we learn how to love from each other. Therefore, educational communities, especially the family, school, and Church, have a special duty to teach sensitivity as the attitude with which we must meet suffering.[170] The pope writes that all educational institutions "must, if only for humanitarian reasons, work perseveringly for the reawakening and refining of that sensitivity toward one's neighbour and his suffering of which the figure of the Good Samaritan in the Gospel has become a symbol."[171]

Imagine how the world might change if we took these words to heart. Perhaps minds and hearts could open to the values that create peace over violence, equality over prejudice, compassion over indifference, and solidarity over division.

Constructing this kind of world permeated with love is the vocation given to us by Jesus in His life-witness and preaching — especially in the parable of the Good Samaritan. It is, indeed, a huge endeavor. Such a society seems idealistic in the face of evil's harsh realities. There are wars being fought, people being slaughtered, and billions who are sick and suffering — it seems we are so far from the goal, and so much is out of control.

But John Paul assures us that the work has already begun and continues in each act of love on behalf of those who suffer. The seeds of charity that we plant will certainly blossom. Consequently, the pope writes, ". . . every individual must feel as if *called personally* to bear witness to love in suffering."[172] Each of us receives this personal invitation from Jesus to model the Good Samaritan and "Go and do likewise" when we encounter suffering.

Following the Master

At the heart of the Gospel call to live as Good Samaritans is the invitation to participate in the ministry of love for sufferers that Jesus himself began. John Paul writes, "The parable of the Good Samaritan is in profound harmony with the conduct of Christ himself."[173] To be a neighbor to others is also to walk in the footsteps of our Master.

Leafing through the Gospels, we need only read a page or two before Jesus' work to comfort sufferers leaps off the page. When Jesus wasn't preaching, He was caring for those who hurt. John Paul writes that Jesus went about "doing good" (Acts 10:38), "and the good of his works became especially evident in the face of human suffering."[174]

This truth comes to life in the numerous biblical accounts of Jesus healing those afflicted by physical and spiritual pain of the worst forms. Jesus cured the paralyzed (Mk. 2:1-12; 3:1-6; Lk. 13:10-17; Jn. 5:1-9), the blind (Mk. 8:22-26; 10:46-52; Jn. 9:1-41), the lepers (Mk. 1:40-45; Lk. 17:11-17), the demonized (Mt. 9:32-33; Mk.1:23-28; 5:1-20; 7:24-30; 9:14-29; Lk. 8:2), and even the dead (Mt. 9:24-25; Lk. 7:14-15; Jn. 11:43-44). The sheer volume of such memories in Scripture testifies to the importance Jesus himself placed on caring for the suffering.

During his life, Jesus brought hope and healing when all people had left was pain and despair. His sensitivity to others' needs catapulted Him into a life of ministry to sufferers, which according to the pope, advanced His Messianic mission foretold by the prophet Isaiah:

> The Spirit of the Lord is upon me, because he has anointed me to preach good news to the poor. He has sent me to proclaim release to the captives and recovering of sight to the blind, to set at liberty those who are oppressed, to proclaim the acceptable year of the Lord.
>
> — Is. 61:1-2[175]

Sufferers witnessed this mission firsthand not only through the awesome power of Jesus' miracles but also through His friendship. An old proverb says you can tell a lot about people by getting to know their friends; this rings especially true when applied to Jesus, because He joined in fellowship with many of those whom society deemed outcasts. They were the shunned and shamed: the poor, the sick, the tax collectors, and the prostitutes. These were people from the wrong side of the tracks — the ones disapproved of by the scribes and Pharisees, who often stood aghast as they watched Jesus and His disciples associate with "these kinds of people."

Nevertheless, Jesus showed himself to be a friend to the friendless. He reached out in compassion to the isolated victims of prejudice and hatred in society. He broke through the discriminatory fences that inflicted pain. And He gave witness in word and deed to the challenging truth that love must burn so ablaze in our hearts that it melts through any walls that keep us apart.

At the same time, the fulfillment of Jesus' Messianic mission required much more than miracles and friendship. It cost Jesus His life, which He laid down for the salvation of a suffering world. As the Lamb of God, Jesus offered himself, as a sacrifice in blood, to cleanse us from the misery of sin and death by which we were sure to perish. From this magnificent act of love sprang the gift of grace and God's promise of eternal life for all who believe.

So it's clear as we flip through the story book of Jesus' life that His love for sufferers defined who He was — a love that we have received and are called, as His disciples, to share. The pope writes:

> If Christ, who knows the interior of man, emphasizes this compassion, this means that it is important for our whole attitude to others' suffering.[176]

An essential step in our own Christian journey is cultivating a Christlike sensitivity to the suffering around us and a disposition of openness that enables us to make a sincere gift of self, as our Lord did.

The Christian tradition gives us a compass to guide us along the way in what have become known as the corporal and spiritual works of mercy. Gleaned from the wisdom of Jesus' teachings and behavior, the works of mercy are specific acts of love we can do to serve as neighbors to those who are hurting.

The corporal works of mercy aim to relieve bodily suffering — feeding the hungry, giving drink to the thirsty, clothing the naked, sheltering the homeless, visiting the sick, ransoming the captive, and burying the dead. The spiritual works of mercy, on the other hand, focus on relieving spiritual suffering — instructing the ignorant, counseling the doubtful, admonishing sinners, bearing wrongs patiently, forgiving offenses willingly, comforting the afflicted, and praying for the living and the dead.

Meditating on these acts of mercy can bear fruits of practical insight and direction that help us put our compassion into action in the spirit of Jesus. We can embark on new vistas of love when we ask, "Where are the hungry, the thirsty, the naked, the homeless, the sick, those in bondage, and the dying in my life, and how can I put on Christ for them? What are the opportunities for me to teach others who long for knowledge, to counsel those in doubt, to lovingly correct sinners, to bear my burdens more patiently, to forgive as Jesus has forgiven me, to comfort those around me who hurt, and to pray for others?" The Church's holiest men and women continue to be those who have considered such questions and then acted on the answers as ministers of mercy.

In trying to make such a response in my own life, I sometimes wish I could be like those first disciples in the Book of Acts who, like Jesus, were able to call down miraculous healings from heaven to help the sick and dying. Peter cured the legs of a man who was lame (3:1), restored the body of a paralyzed man who had been bedridden for eight years (9:14), and even healed multitudes of people who merely fell in his shadow (5:14). Phillip exorcised demons and healed the sick in Samaria (8:7), while Paul cured a man plagued by fever and dysentery (28:8-9).

Miracles like these, worked through the apostles' hands, brought the compassionate touch of Jesus to those who were cured in such powerful ways. I think about how wonderful it would be if I could express my mercy like that — empowered by God's might to heal the many people I meet who are broken by suffering. However, for me and for most of us, this is a foreign experience well beyond the realm of understanding. Barring a special grace given by God, we can't express our love through the miraculous.

Fortunately, Jesus doesn't ask us to. Instead, He calls us to roll up our sleeves to help our brothers and sisters in whatever ways we can. We're never quite sure what the results of our work might be. We don't have any assurances of success. Sometimes we'll come to know the joy of healing and bringing peace to those who suffer. In other cases, all of the hard work and personal sacrifice will seem to yield little or no measurable result. It just goes to prove that we, like the Good Samaritan, have to make that leap of faith as we reach out to those who need us.

Undoubtedly, love, as an action-oriented virtue, strives for results. To be a neighbor of love is to work to make the suffering of another go away, or at least improve. At the same time, we also have to recognize the obvious — we're not God. Because we're human, our help will always be limited by earthly constraints like time, money, knowledge, and even sin. We can't erase these obstacles completely from our lives or the human landscape. But by God's grace, we can work together to find effective ways around them to bring help to those who are hurting. We can cultivate a keener vision of others' needs. We can seize opportunities to serve our brothers and sisters. In doing so, we live as Good Samaritans and disciples of Jesus, who continue His work to overcome the brutality of suffering in the world with the tender gift of love.

In his reflections on the parable of the Good Samaritan, John Paul reminds us that the positive Christian understanding of suffering as a way to participate in the saving ministry of Jesus in no way justifies neglect of those who need our care. Although suffering has been redeemed by the Cross, and therefore can become something good for us in the Church, it is still an experience of evil that brings anguish and tears.

Thus, we can't stand by idly and allow others to suffer by assuming it is God's will or spiritually good for them. As the pope has reminded us, we must respond to suffering with love and care in the spirit of the Good Samaritan, for being loving neighbors defines our moral lives as followers of Jesus, whose ministry of good works on behalf of the suffering lights our way.

Enlightened by these truths about suffering as God has revealed them to us, John Paul concludes:

> At one and the same time Christ has taught man *to do good by his suffering* and *to do good to those who suffer.* In this double aspect he has completely revealed the meaning of suffering.[177]

ACKNOWLEDGEMENTS

I humbly express my gratitude to His Holiness, the late Pope John Paul II, whose insightful and sensitive words on the Christian meaning of suffering inspired this book. Reflecting at length on the pope's wisdom has been a great blessing, and I feel privileged to have been his student during this project.

My deepest and heartfelt thanks go to my beautiful wife, Sarah, whose love and countless sacrifices enabled me to write the book. I'm grateful for her encouragement to follow my calling and for the many creative ideas she contributed during our conversations about content. I thank her also for giving me an honest critique of my words and for working night and day to create time for me to write. These are special gifts for which I'm most indebted.

I want to say thanks to my lovely little girl, Elizabeth, whose giggles and hugs made me smile when writing didn't come easy, and to my family — especially my mom, Terry, and my mother- and father-in-law, Roberta and Barry Polley, who logged many babysitting hours to help me find extra writing time. Thanks also to my cousin and good friend, Joe Hengehold, for intelligent dialog about the ideas in this book over countless cups of coffee.

Finally, I want to express my appreciation to Michael Dubruiel and Janet Butler at Our Sunday Visitor for their guidance and enthusiasm about this book, Jeff Hillard for his wise counsel about matters of literary marketing, and Paul Jenkins and his staff at the College of Mount St. Joseph Library, for kindly providing me with ample resources for my research and a quiet haven in which to write.

ENDNOTES

1. *Gaudium et Spes*, 22, in *Salvifici Doloris*, VIII:31

2. Pope John Paul II, *Salvifici Doloris* (Washington, DC: United States Catholic Conference, February 1984), I:2

3. Pope John Paul II, "Join Your Suffering to Christ's," in *The Loving Heart: The Private Prayers of Pope John Paul II* (New York, NY: Atria Books, 2005), 46

4. *Salvifici Doloris*, II:6

5. Ibid., I:3

6. Ibid., IV:15

7. John Milton, *Paradise Lost*, ed. Scott Elledge (New York, NY: W.W. Norton & Company, 1975), Book XI.461-465, 253

8. Ibid., Book XI.480-482, 253

9. Ibid., Book XI.500-507, 253-254

10. *The Loving Heart,* 37

11. *Gaudium et Spes*, 37

12. *Salvifici Doloris*, II:7

13. Ibid.

14. Ibid.

15. Ibid.

16. Ibid., II:5

17. René Laurentin, *Bernadette of Lourdes*, trans. John Dury (Minneapolis, MN: Winston Press, 1979), 55

18. Ibid., 231

19. *Salvifici Doloris*, II:5

20. Ibid.

21. Ibid., II:6

22. *Dark Night of the Soul*, trans., ed. E. Allison Peers, 3rd rev. ed. (New York, NY: Doubleday, 1990), 115

23. Lam. 3:8; also cf. *Dark Night of the Soul*, 115

24. Saint Faustina, *Diary of Saint Maria Faustina Kowalska: Divine Mercy in My Soul*, 3rd ed. (Stockbridge, MA: Marian Press, 2004), 55

25. *Salvifici Doloris*, II:6

26. Rev. Jim Willig, *Lessons from the School of Suffering* (Cincinnati, OH: St. Anthony Messenger Press, 2001), 48

27. *Salvifici Doloris*, II:6

28. Ibid.

29. Archbishop Fulton Sheen, "Philosophy of Anxiety," in *Peace of Soul* (Liguori, MO: Triumph Books, 1949), 15

30. *The Loving Heart*, 46

31. Ibid., 51

32. Pope John Paul II, "*Mysterium mortis*" in *Sign of Contradiction* (New York, NY: Seabury Press, 1979), 156-158

33. *Salvifici Doloris*, II:7

34. Ibid.

35. Ibid., II:8

36. Ibid.

37. Ibid.

38. Ibid., II:7

39. Ibid., II:8

40. Ibid.

41. Ibid.

42. Ibid.

43. Ibid.

44. Ibid.

45. Ibid., III:9

46. Ibid.

47. G.K. Chesterton, "On Original Sin," in *Come to Think of It . . . A Book of Essays* (London: Methuen & Co. Ltd., 1930), 155

48. *The Loving Heart*, 43

49. Ibid.

50. Ibid.

51. Clifford Geertz, *The Interpretation of Cultures* (New York, NY: Basic Books, 1973), 103

52. Peter Devries, *The Blood of the Lamb* (Boston, MA: Little, Brown & Company, 1961), 215

53. Ibid.

54. Ibid., 243

55. *The Loving Heart*, 39

56. *Salvifici Doloris*, III:9

57. Ibid., III:10

58. Fyodor Dostoyevsky, *The Brothers Karamazov*, trans. Constance Garnett (New York, NY: New American Library, 1999), 235

59. *The Loving Heart*, 38

60. C.S. Lewis, *A Grief Observed* (New York, NY: Seabury Press, 1961), 9-10

61. *The Loving Heart*, 38

62. Ibid.

63. *Salvifici Doloris*, III:10

64. Ibid., III:10

65. Ibid.

66. Ibid.

67. Ibid., III:10

68. Ibid., III:10

69. Ibid., III:12

70. Ibid., III:11

71. Ibid., III:12

72. Ibid., III:11

73. Ibid.

74. Ibid.

75. Ibid.

76. Ibid.

77. Ibid.

78. Ibid.

79. Ibid., III:12

80. Ibid., III:13

81. Ibid.

82. Ibid., IV:14

83. Ibid.

84. Ibid.

85. Ibid.

86. Medard Kehl and Werner Loser, eds. *The Von Balthasar Reader,* trans. Robert J. Daly and Fred Lawrence (New York, NY: Crossroad, 1982), 148

87. Karl Rahner, S.J. *Theological Investigations, vol. 21*, trans. Hugh M. Riley (New York, NY: Crossroad, 1988), 250

88. *Salvifici Doloris*, IV:17

89. Ibid.

90. Ibid., IV:14

91. Ibid., IV:17

92. Ibid.

93. Ibid., IV:16

94. Ibid.

95. Ibid., IV:15

96. Ibid.

97. Ibid., VI:15

98. Ibid.

99. Ibid., III:15

100. Ibid., IV:15

101. Ibid., VI:15

102. Elie Wiesel, *Night* (New York, NY: Bantam, 1982), 62

103. *Salvifici Doloris*, V:22

104. Ibid., IV:16

105. Ibid., IV:18

106. Ibid.

107. Gustavo Gutierrez, *On Job: God-Talk and the Suffering of the Innocent*, trans. Matthew J. O'Connell (New York, NY: Orbis Books, 1987), 101

108. *Salvifici Doloris*, IV:18

109. Ibid., VI:25

110. Ibid.

111. Ibid., VI:25

112. Ibid., IV:25

113. St. Ignatius of Antioch, *Letter to the Romans*, In Rev. John Laux, *Church History* (Rockford, IL: TAN Books, 1989), 50

114. St. Ignatius of Antioch, *Letter to the Romans*, in William A. Jurgens, *Faith of the Early Fathers,* vol. 1 (Collegeville, MN: Liturgical Press, 1970), 21-22

115. Tertullian, *Apolog. 50*, in Rev. John Laux, *Church History* (Rockford, IL: TAN Books, 1989), 48

116. Pope John Paul II, *Tertio Millennio Adveniente* (Washington, DC: United States Catholic Conference), 10

117. Paul Marshal, *Their Blood Cries Out* (Dallas, TX: Word Publishing, 1997)

118. *Salvifici Doloris*, V:22

119. Ibid., VI:26

120. Ibid., V:24

121. Ibid., V:20

122. Ibid., V:19

123. Ibid., V:24

124. Ibid.

125. Ibid.

126. Ibid.

127. Ibid.

128. Ibid.

129. Ibid.

130. Ibid., VI:27

131. Ibid.

132. Hans Urs von Balthasar, "Bought at a Great Price," in *You Crown the Year with Your Goodness* (San Francisco, CA: Ignatius, 1989), 81

133. *Salvifici Doloris*, VI:26

134. Ibid.

135. Ibid., VI:27

136. Ibid.

137. St. Thérèse of Lisieux, *St. Thérèse of Lisieux: Her Last Conversations*, trans. John Clarke, O.C.D. (Washington, DC: Institute of Carmelite Studies, 1977), 123

138. *Salvifici Doloris*, VI:26

139. Mother Teresa, *No Greater Love*, eds. Becky Benenate and Joseph Durepos (Novato, CA, New World Library, 1997), 136-137

140. *Salvifici Doloris*, VI:27

141. Ibid., VI:26

142. Ibid.

143. Ibid.

144. *Gaudium et Spes*, 24, in *Salvifici Doloris*, VIII:31

145. *Salvifici Doloris*, VII:30

146. Ibid.

147. *Salvifici Doloris*, VII:29

148. Ibid., VII:28

149. Ibid., VI:28

150. Ibid., VII:28

151. Ibid.

152. Ibid.

153. Ibid.

154. Ibid.

155. Ibid.

156. Ibid., VII:29

157. Ibid.

158. Ibid.

159. *Gaudium et Spes*, 24, in *Salvifici Doloris*, VII:29

160. *Salvifici Doloris*, VII:29

161. Mother Teresa, *No Greater Love*, eds. Becky Benenate, Joseph Durepos (Novato, CA: New World Library, 1989), 88-89

162. *Salvifici Doloris*, VII:30

163. Ibid., VII:28

164. Dorothy Day, "Love Is the Measure," in *Dorothy Day: Selected Writings*, ed. Robert Ellsberg (Maryknoll, NY: Orbis Books, 1992), 98

165. *Salvifici Doloris*, VII:30
166. Ibid., VII:29
167. Ibid.
168. Ibid.
169. Ibid.
170. Ibid., VII:30
171. Ibid.
172. Ibid., VII:29
173. Ibid., VII:30
174. Ibid., VII:30
175. Referred to in *Salvifici Doloris*, VII:30
176. Ibid., VII:28
177. Ibid., VII:30